MW00488974

Fieldwork

An Expeditionary Learning
Outward Bound
Reader

Volume II

Edited by
Amy Mednick
Emily Cousins

KENDALL/HUNT PUBLISHING COMPANY
4050 Westmark Drive   Dubuque, Iowa 52002

On the front cover:

Kindergartners Lauren Rutherford, Aimee Moyer, and Jackie Phillips of the Rocky Mountain School for Expeditionary Learning in Denver take a moment to read together on a sofa in class. (top left)

Keith Studmire, a middle school student at the Rafael Hernandez School in Boston, builds a straw structure as part of a service learning, architecture expedition. (top right)

Student Lucas Tamayo of the Rafael Hernandez School in Boston holds up a magnified ant collected during a learning expedition on insects. (bottom left)

Tim Cronin, a science teacher at King Middle School in Portland, Maine, examines a shell with seventh-grade students Nicole Kangas and Kristin Lapin for the learning expedition "The Ocean: What's Under There?" (bottom right)

Photographs by David Cornwell. Cover design concept by Casey Cheung.

Expeditionary Learning℠ is a Service Mark of Outward Bound, Inc.

Outward Bound© is a Registered Trademark of Outward Bound, Inc.

Dedicated to Harold "Doc" Howe II who, with humility and puckish humor, provides us with vision and leadership.

Contents

Preface
Powerful Learning Experiences

What was your most powerful learning experience between preschool and high school graduation? I have asked that question many times to teachers, administrators, and parents in the three years since we began Expeditionary Learning Outward Bound. The answers have always contained the two elements the late educator and scholar Paul Ylvisaker said were the prerequisite to learning: challenge and emotion.

One of the startling discoveries about asking so many people this question is how infrequently the answers arise from their experiences in the classroom. I have never had anyone tell me that his or her most powerful learning experience as a child or adolescent was completing a worksheet or listening to a teacher lecture. Every story has the student as the main character doing something hard, something he or she was not quite sure he or she would be able to do. Sometimes the story is about the lessons learned from failure, and the perseverance that came on the heels of that failure.

Caring adults feature prominently as teachers, coaches, ministers, camp and scout leaders who provided support and challenge in these memories. The memories are often of a shared experience with a small group of peers. When the powerful learning experience remembered is school-based, it often took place outside the school day as an extracurricular activity—whether it was a sport, band, play, or service. Saturdays and Sundays and after school were rich with learning too.

Given that students spend most of their school day in classrooms, and the express purpose of going to the classroom is to learn, it is striking that, as adults, looking back on our own education, so few of us single out that dominant experience as the springboard to our most powerful learning experiences. Those classrooms that do get noted tend to be the ones where the memory swirls around a very special year with a particular teacher who made a deep connection with us.

We have set a difficult mission for ourselves as we seek to teach in ways very different from the ways we may have been taught ourselves. We seek to organize our schools in ways that will promote and support students' having many powerful learning experiences within their school day. We ask our students to revise their work until it is of a quality that they determine warrants preserving for their own grandchildren. We want our time with our students to matter now and for the rest of their lives. We want our time together to matter to them just as it matters to us.

How do we design powerful learning experiences for our classrooms and schools? We turn to our ten design principles: The Primacy of Self-Discovery; The Having of Wonderful Ideas; The Responsibility for Learning; Intimacy and Caring; Success and Failure; Collaboration and Competition; Diversity and Inclusivity; The Natural World; Solitude and Reflection; and Service and Compassion. When teaching is organized and prioritized with evidence of these design principles, powerful learning experiences will result.

Yes, we are inventing and designing new ways of teaching and organizing our schools and classrooms, schools, and school systems. This book, *Fieldwork, Volume II* grows out of those efforts, including selections from our monthly newsletter *The Web*, as well as other reprints. This second volume of *Fieldwork* is enriched by the expertise and experience of educators—from classrooms to the wilderness—from across the country. Together, we are committed to documenting the sometimes quicksilver, often difficult process of educational reform. We offer *Fieldwork, Volume II* in the spirit of collaboration as well as deep appreciation to educators who continue to share their craft wisdom with a wider audience.

Reaching back to the wellspring of our powerful learning experiences places us at the beginning of our own journeys as passionate learners. When we return to our own roots and remember the way we learned best, it is easier to envision our classrooms and schools as centers of Expeditionary Learning. What we must continue to do to make them so is challenging because schools have not traditionally been organized around these design principles. But once we remember how we learned best, we owe our students nothing less.

—Meg Campbell
June 1996

Acknowledgments

We are especially grateful to New American Schools for its generous support and guidance. We thank the following funders who have made our work possible: Americorps, the DeWitt Wallace-Readers' Digest Foundation, the J.M. Kaplan Fund, the Geraldine R. Dodge Foundation, the Edna McConnell Clark Foundation, the Dragon Foundation, the Surdna Foundation, and the Starr Foundation.

We thank our partner school districts in Boston, Massachusetts; Cincinnati, Ohio; Decatur, Georgia; Dubuque, Iowa; Denver, Colorado; Memphis, Tennessee; New York, New York; Portland, Maine; and San Antonio, Texas. Special thanks also to the administrators, teachers, parents, and students at our collaborating schools who contributed to this book in many significant ways, including writing articles, providing illustrations, being interviewed or photographed, and taking responsibility for the mundane but essential administrative tasks involved in bringing a book to publication.

We thank the following people for giving their time and support in the development of this book: Vivian Fung, Guiomar Garcia, Daphne Leslie Harris, Leah Rugen, Patricia Sarango, Margo Shearman, and Denis Udall. Special thanks to Casey Cheung who, during his internship, lent creativity, organizational abilities, and meticulous attention to detail. Finally, we acknowledge our colleagues at Expeditionary Learning Outward Bound who, through their vision, dedication, and hard work, made this book possible.

Introduction

Greg Farrell

We looked up "expedition" in the dictionary, and the first definition given there was "a journey with a purpose." Well, we're about to start off on an expedition together, and its purpose for each of you is to be open to the experience and the things there are to learn out there.

—Victoria Woodhull, a Hurricane Island
Outward Bound program director addressing
teachers leaving on an Outward Bound course.

This is a book of vivid examples and practical reflections. Reading it is like picking your way through a field of growing things. It is rich with the day-to-day experiences and ideas of teachers and students teaching and learning in a new old-fashioned way: by doing things and then thinking about them. It is full of discoveries and brushes with reality and honest thoughts about the experience of teaching. It is made up of the testimonies of people who have opened themselves to the experience of teaching in an active mode. It is a partial record of what they and their students are learning from the experience.

Fieldwork, Volume II is an appropriate name for this book, because its purpose is to ground the reader in the particulars of active learning. Written primarily by teachers, this book is the second in a series of stories from the field. Eleanor Duckworth, in her classes at the Harvard Graduate School of Education, uses the term fieldwork for what students do outside of class to dig deeper into the material they wrestle with in class. It is a form of homework, but it has the subtly different implication that students will probably not be doing it in the library or at their desks. Instead, they will be trying things out and thinking for themselves.

There are about twenty-five Expeditionary Learning schools in various stages of development as this

book goes to press. The work of these schools gives rise to this book. In these schools—elementary, middle, and high schools in nine different parts of the country—fieldwork takes students out of the classroom and into contact with the world. Scott Gill, who works both for the Dubuque, Iowa, public schools and Expeditionary Learning Outward Bound, is fond of saying that this kind of teaching and learning replaces the old field *trips* with field *work*. There are no more boring bus trips, he says, for twenty-five or thirty youngsters to visit a sewage treatment plant or the local newspaper. Instead, as a part of a larger intellectual expedition, one or two or three students at a time go out to interview the manager of the treatment plant and several of the workers, or they spend the day with the circulation manager of the newspaper. They have thought out in advance what questions they want to ask and what they want to find out. It is not a trip; it is work. Perhaps it is the central part of their work the way a community survey is for a pollster or a dig is for an archeologist.

Learning things by doing them is the oldest and best way of learning them. For some things, like learning to ski or play the violin, it is the only way. But for reasons too complicated to go into in this introduction, we have moved away from learning by doing in schools and have separated the means of education from the ends, boring most of our students and making pretenders of most of our teachers in the process. Expeditionary Learning Outward Bound is just one of several contemporary educational reform efforts that seek to improve teaching and learning by making it more active, building it around projects and fieldwork, and holding it to standards of social purpose and practical consequence that pass muster in the community at large.

Teaching and learning this way is exhilarating and rewarding, but it is also hard work. And it is risky, since it differs from business as usual in most schools. Teachers find it new and scary to leave old ways and try new ones, and we hear this anxiety in the following articles. The educators who contributed to this book have one major advantage, however. Because their schools and school districts have embraced Expeditionary Learning, they have parent, school, and district support for their work. But still the larger system of incentives and rewards and sanctions does not always support them. The teachers and administrators whose work appears in the pages of this book then, are ground-breakers in pioneering school districts. We hope this book will help make their work less unusual, their approach the common approach, and their schools and districts lightships helping to show the way for others.

The particular work that generates this book is rooted not only in practice, but in principle. Expeditionary Learning, a project of Outward Bound, is a framework for school reform based primarily on the educational and developmental insights of Kurt Hahn, the German English educator who founded Outward Bound, the Atlantic Colleges, the Duke of Edinburgh Awards, the Salem School in Germany and the Gordonstoun School in Scotland. Hahn insisted that his educational ideas were not original: he borrowed freely from Plato and William James and the educational reformers of his own time. He believed that character held greater importance than knowledge. He described self-discovery as the first principle of education, and wrote that it was achieved most profoundly in the pursuit of the common good. The teachers' first responsibility was to help their students find their "grand passions" and pursue them to levels of mastery, and at the same time help them make real progress in their areas of weakness.

The Expeditionary Learning project has taken Hahn's "Seven Laws of Salem," the principles by which he organized and led his first school, and added to them from more than fifty years of Outward Bound's experience with students and teachers around the world and from the insights of more modern educators like Eleanor Duckworth and Paul Ylvisaker to arrive at ten design principles for creating schools where character development and academic achievement are equally important. This book comes then, not only from encounters with a new manifestation of an old-fashioned kind of teaching practice, but from wrestling at the same time with some old-fashioned principles that have to do not only with teaching and learning, but with what it means to be human.

Greg Farrell is the president of Expeditionary Learning Outward Bound, and vice president for Urban Educational Programs for Outward Bound USA.

Expeditionary Learning Outward Bound®
Design Principles

Learning is an expedition into the unknown. Expeditions draw together personal experience and intellectual growth to promote self-discovery and construct knowledge. We believe that adults should guide students along this journey with care, compassion, and respect for their diverse learning styles, backgrounds, and needs. Addressing individual differences profoundly increases the potential for learning and creativity of each student.

Given fundamental levels of health, safety, and love, all people can and want to learn. We believe expeditionary learning harnesses the natural passion to learn and is a powerful method for developing the curiosity, skills, knowledge, and courage needed to imagine a better world and work toward realizing it.

1. The Primacy of Self-Discovery

Learning happens best with emotion, challenge, and the requisite support. People discover their abilities, values, "grand passions," and responsibilities in situations that offer adventure and the unexpected. They must have tasks that require perseverance, fitness, craftsmanship, imagination, self-discipline, and significant achievement. A primary job of the educator is to help students overcome their fear and discover they have more in them than they think.

2. The Having of Wonderful Ideas

Teach so as to build on children's curiosity about the world by creating learning situations that provide matter to think about, time to experiment, and time to make sense of what is observed. Foster a community where students' and adults' ideas are respected.

3. The Responsibility for Learning

Learning is both a personal, individually specific process of discovery and a social activity. Each of us learns within and for ourselves and as a part of a group. Every aspect of a school must encourage children, young people, and adults to become increasingly responsible for directing their own personal and collective learning.

4. Intimacy and Caring

Learning is fostered best in small groups where there is trust, sustained caring and mutual respect among all members of the learning community. Keep schools and learning groups small. Be sure there is a caring adult looking after the progress of each child. Arrange for the older students to mentor the younger ones.

5. Success and Failure

All students must be assured a fair measure of success in learning in order to nurture the confidence and capacity to take risks and rise to increasingly difficult challenges. But it is also important to experience failure, to overcome negative inclinations, to prevail against adversity, and to learn to turn disabilities into opportunities.

6. Collaboration and Competition

Teach so as to join individual and group development so that the value of friendship, trust, and group endeavor is made manifest. Encourage students to compete, not against each other, but with their own personal best and with rigorous standards of excellence.

7. Diversity and Inclusivity

Diversity and inclusivity in all groups dramatically increases richness of ideas, creative power, problem-solving ability, and acceptance of others. Encourage students to investigate, value, and draw upon their own different histories, talents, and resources together with those of other communities and cultures. Keep the schools and learning groups heterogeneous.

8. The Natural World

A direct and respectful relationship with the natural world refreshes the human spirit and reveals the important lessons of recurring cycles and cause and effect. Students learn to become stewards of the earth and of the generations to come.

9. Solitude and Reflection

Solitude, reflection, and silence replenish our energies and open our minds. Be sure students have time alone to explore their own thoughts, make their own connections, and create their own ideas. Then give them opportunity to exchange their reflections with each other and with adults.

10. Service and Compassion

We are crew, not passengers, and are strengthened by acts of consequential service to others. One of a school's primary functions is to prepare its students with the attitudes and skills to learn from and be of service to others.

The above principles have been informed by Kurt Hahn's "Seven Laws of Salem," by Paul Ylvisaker's "The Missing Dimension," and by Eleanor Duckworth's *"The Having of Wonderful Ideas" and Other Essays on Teaching and Learning* (New York: Teachers College Press, Columbia University, 1987).

Part One

Learning Expeditions

Now instead of reading everything from a textbook we go out and do stuff on field trips, or like on our pond expedition, we didn't just read about the microorganisms we actually went out to different ponds and got specimens.

—Journal Entry
Ben Wilson, fifth grade
Table Mound Elementary School
Dubuque

Characteristics of Learning Expeditions:
Expanding the Dialogue

This effort at capturing some of the key attributes of learning expeditions draws heavily from the experience and ideas of Expeditionary Learning Outward Bound teachers and school designers. It is also inspired by three of our most influential mentors: Kurt Hahn, Eleanor Duckworth, and Thomas James. We offer these ideas in the spirit of contributing to our network's growing conversation about learning expeditions and the nature of teaching and learning.

A Community of Learners

Just as an expedition to a remote mountain range requires its members to prepare carefully and pool their efforts, learning expeditions call upon learners to collaborate intensely on goals in which they are all deeply invested. Students work toward shared goals and outcomes that can only be accomplished by drawing upon the talents, passions, and efforts of the entire group. The founder of Outward Bound, Kurt Hahn, keenly understood the educational power of small groups. He believed that in intimate settings leadership abilities can emerge that are present but inhibited in most people. Moreover, Hahn believed that through shared commitment a genuine community begins to take shape. As Thomas James commented, Hahn saw one of the key aims of schools was to "harmonize the social and intellectual differences between students by operating as a community of participation and active service . . ." where students mediate their own personal goals within a larger purpose.

A Journey into the Unknown

An expedition is a journey into the unknown. There is something intriguing and inviting yet mysterious about the way it opens up before you; the deeper you are drawn into it, the more the terrain reveals itself. The searching questions and problems that illuminate an expedition from within call upon learners to examine their hypotheses, ideas, and beliefs. A search for creative solutions and a willingness to

Students work toward shared goals and outcomes that can only be accomplished by drawing upon the talents, passions, and efforts of the entire group.

confront formidable problems and to examine ideas from a variety of perspectives guide the inquiry and elude the search for one right answer. The questions learners ask themselves and others provide pathways into subject matter. Expeditionary content is meaningful to learners because they lend their intelligence to it: they grapple with problems, questions, and dilemmas of their own making. Thus, expeditions are built around subject matter complex enough that it elicits multidimensional hypotheses, and problem-solving strategies and approaches.

Crew, Not Passengers

Young people learn best when they are allowed to use their formidable energies in service of the common good. "You are crew, not passengers," Kurt Hahn said when he directed his first school in Germany. Just as there are times during an expedition when each individual takes his or her own personal initiative, so there are opportunities for students to subdue their own personal interests in pursuit of a larger purpose that teaches them the bonds of social life. Students' projects should include opportunities for adults and others to depend on the actions of young people and should address problems or issues that both students and the community believe are important and worthwhile. Hahn declared, "Let the responsible boys and girls shoulder duties big enough, when negligently performed, to wreck the State."

Peak Performance

History's great expeditions have always sought difficult, seemingly unattainable prizes or destinations, ones that were worthy of their efforts. Achieving the goal required arduous, complicated work that endowed it with tremendous meaning and an aura of mystique. Learning expeditions should aim for summits that appear to exceed what could reasonably be expected of students.

Learner as Apprentice

An Outward Bound course begins with an instructor teaching her students the content and skills required to navigate unfamiliar terrain. The teacher models strategies embedded in real-world applications. Then the teacher guides students in attempting tasks. Near the end of the expedition, students continue on their own, as the instructor fades into the background and supports them from afar. Learning expeditions are similarly designed. Teachers enable students to work independently. They constantly ask themselves, "Am I doing something for my students that they could be doing for themselves?" Their goal is for their students to bring to bear all the knowledge and skills they have mastered

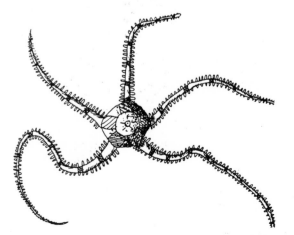

Nick Zaccaro, a seventh-grade student at King Middle School in Portland, Maine, drew the Daisy Brittle Star as his contribution to a field guide to the Gulf of Maine.

to carry out a culminating expedition that requires them to collaborate with their peers, as well as work on their own.

Overcoming Limits

To experience only an unbroken chain of more limited successes that never challenge or strengthen the human spirit is not nearly as valuable as learning to push beyond our perceived limitations for a worthy cause or for another human being. Learning expeditions help to develop young people's capacity for positive action, but also for overcoming constraints within themselves to surmount obstacles in their academic achievement. In doing so, expeditions teach persistence in turning disability into opportunity and weakness into strength.

Learning expeditions help to develop young people's capacity for positive action, but also for overcoming constraints within themselves to surmount obstacles in their academic achievement.

A Sense of Where You Are

No expedition leaves port without a strong sense of where it is going and without pausing along the way to take its bearings. But rarely do expeditions know the lay of the land they are about to explore before they set out. So they must build in frequent opportunities for self-correction and evaluation to stay their course. Expeditionary Learning classrooms strive to establish an ethic where sustained work toward clear, high standards is the norm, and in which discussing, conferring, revising, critiquing, and reflecting become common practice. There is explicit emphasis on effort, perseverance, and doing one's personal best. By providing lots of opportunities for learners to take stock of where they are in relation to the standards they have set for themselves, expeditions place success within students' reach. ◆

A Framework for Planning a Learning Expedition

I. What Is a Learning Expedition?

Definition: A form of curriculum design (pre-K–12) in which teachers and students pursue long-term intellectual investigations built around significant projects and performances. The investigations take students out into the world and bring the world into the classroom. Often they provide students with opportunities to serve the wider community. The learning expedition is marked by equal attention to goals of academic content and performance, and character development and community. Opportunities for ongoing assessment are woven throughout the expedition, pushing students to higher levels of achievement.

A. General Qualities (Underlying Principles):

◆ A strong connection to the world, inside and outside the classroom—a focus on linking the classroom and the outside world, fully drawing on school and community resources.

◆ Teachers possess a passion for learning and alertness to opportunity, and endeavor to help their students share the same.

◆ High standards and stakes—an emphasis on student work of consequence, quality, and value in major projects, as well as ongoing, smaller tasks and assignments.

◆ Expanding time and space to make room for in-depth expeditions, fieldwork, teachers' collaboration, and multidisciplinary connections.

◆ Leadership and organization on the part of teachers and students.

◆ New roles for learners—images of groups of students as crews, and individual students as explorers and apprentices.

◆ A clear focus on assessment and understanding—fostering a continuous process of reflection, critique, and revision among teachers and students. Everyone is constantly asking, "How am I doing?"

Snorkeling in the Gulf of Maine, students at King Middle School, with science teacher Tim Cronin, discover "What's Under There" in an expedition on the ocean. Photograph by David Cornwell.

B. Key Components/Entry Points in Planning:

- ◆ Theme/topic
- ◆ Guiding questions
- ◆ Clear set of learning goals (consistent with school, district, or state guidelines)
- ◆ Major/final project as an assessment task

II. Suggestions for Organizing a Learning Expedition Plan

(A "plan" is a written document outlining your plans for the learning expedition.)

Planning learning expeditions is a creative and collaborative process for which every group will develop its personal approach. The following questions are presented to stimulate and support your work.

A. What is the *theme* or *topic* of your learning expedition?

The focus and content of the learning expedition should include the most important ideas and concepts from your discipline(s) that you, as a teacher, believe all students must understand deeply. What background knowledge and skills will students need to develop and use in order to produce strong work in the expedition? What big ideas will students grapple with, and are they important to know? Will students have ample opportunity to use different modes of inquiry?

The Horned Lizard has horns on the back of his head. The horns give the animal a fierce look. Most horned lizards lay from six to forty eggs at a time.
—*Nolan Heins, a second-grade
student at Table Mound Elementary School in Dubuque, Iowa.*

- ◆ The theme/topic of a learning expedition should be rich and complex enough to support well-developed guiding questions. It should also be concrete enough to be accessible to students' experience and interests.
- ◆ A good theme/topic allows the learning expedition to encompass more than one discipline and make connections across fields of knowledge.

B. What are the *guiding questions* that you hope to explore with the students through this learning expedition?

Learning expeditions begin with thought-provoking, searching questions that provide pathways into subject matter. The questions are often big and overarching, and guide the inquiry into a particular content area. For example, the question "What separates humans from other animals?" can lead into a learning expedition on the animal kingdom. Or the question "How do we create a just society?" can lead into a learning expedition on justice or government. However, these big questions quickly lead to derivative questions that are more tightly focused ("Is language a uniquely human form of communication?" "What responsibilities should a government have to its citizens? And what responsibilities should people have to their government?"). Bear in mind that seemingly simple, mundane topics such as "bugs," "kites," or "pond life" can lead to rich and important questions, many of which will be generated by the students themselves.

Good guiding questions

- ◆ ask students to solve or investigate an interesting problem or dilemma, or make a decision about an important issue or problem
- ◆ probe deeply and challenge students to think critically
- ◆ ask students to explore important ideas, problems, and methods of inquiry that lie at the heart of a discipline or a domain of knowledge
- ◆ are open-ended (no "one right answer"), provocative, and controversial
- ◆ are meaningful (or can be made meaningful) to students

Kindergartners from the Rafael Hernandez School in Boston collect ants at a nearby park during an expedition on insects. Photograph by David Cornwell.

C. What are your *learning goals*?

At the close of this learning expedition, what do you want your students

- ◆ to know (content)
- ◆ to be able to do (performance)
- ◆ to be like (dispositions)

Learning expeditions involve in-depth inquiry. They ask students to

- ◆ view issues and problems from a variety of perspectives (Whose viewpoint are we seeing? What other viewpoints might there be if we changed perspectives?)
- ◆ look for evidence; evaluate for bias (What's my evidence for what I believe? How credible is it?)
- ◆ draw upon their prior knowledge
- ◆ examine, analyze, and investigate relationships among different ideas, people, events, concepts, and phenomena (How is one thing connected to another? Is there a pattern here?)
- ◆ connect what they are learning to the real world[1]

[1] Some of these ideas are drawn from the "Habits of Mind" developed by Central Park East Secondary School and the Coalition of Essential Schools.

A good learning expedition provides opportunities for students to communicate their ideas. Students should be able to

- ◆ use multiple resources to create and present strong written and oral work
- ◆ organize their ideas in a clear, coherent, and convincing way
- ◆ use persuasive, lively, and descriptive language
- ◆ construct original products and express themselves through a variety of artistic genres
- ◆ present and explain their work to a discerning audience

Learning expeditions also foster strong work habits (such as organization, perseverance, planning, and follow-through) and strong working relationships (for example, listening, sharing ideas, trust, and compassion).

D. What ideas do you have for *projects* within this learning expedition?

Projects are composed of a variety of products, tasks, and/or demonstrations that students carry out both individually and in groups, including opportunities for fieldwork and service.

Learning expeditions leave room for student choice in determining and shaping projects.

Good projects

◆ ask the seemingly impossible of students
◆ provide a compelling application for an academically rigorous body of knowledge and skills
◆ include a balance of group and individual tasks, allowing individual students to stretch beyond their perceived limits
◆ are broken down into discrete components to provide frequent checkpoints for teachers to monitor student progress and for students to engage in the ongoing assessment of their own work and that of their peers
◆ confront students with real-world problems and emulate the approaches, materials, language, and standards that professionals in the world outside of school would use to solve those problems
◆ engage students with a rich variety of resources (for instance, books, maps, models, poetry, primary sources, paintings, sculptures, murals, and music; software programs, films, and videos; and experts, companies, and neighborhood organizations)

E. How will you *assess* to what extent the goals for the learning expedition have been met?

Throughout the learning expedition, ongoing assessment

◆ includes opportunities for students to assess and evaluate their work against clear standards at many different junctures
◆ includes critique sessions, peer revision, conferences, discussions of the qualities of good work by examining exemplars, and development of standards and criteria for what makes good work

Lisa Jacobson, art teacher at the School for the Physical City in New York City, works on a mural with student Sherman Barr. Photograph by Carrie Boretz for the New York Times.

◆ allows time for individual reflection in between assessment activities

◆ provides teachers with opportunities to reflect on and make adjustments to their practice

◆ culminates with an exhibition, demonstration, performance, or portfolio review that gives students a chance to knit together what they have learned and to display their learning to an outside audience; such culminating exhibitions call upon students to demonstrate the most important ideas, knowledge, and performances they *must* know and be able to do

F. A few final considerations for developing a learning expedition:

◆ What is the time line or projected sequence?

◆ What are the ideas for opening/kick-off activities?

◆ What are the ideas for incorporating service into the expedition?

◆ Is there a role for parents in the planning, implementation, and assessment of the expedition?

◆ How will the design principles be reflected in this learning expedition? ◆

Lauren Rutherford, a kindergartner at the Rocky Mountain School of Expeditionary Learning in Denver, enjoys a storybook. Photograph by David Cornwell.

Universal Questions:
Astronomy Learning Expeditions

Amy Mednick

This feature is meant to give readers insight into what teachers believe worked and did not work in particular learning expeditions, and also to give practical suggestions for contacts, resources, and reading materials. We focus on a sampling of astronomy learning expeditions taught at the Rafael Hernandez School in Boston, and at Bryant and Table Mound elementary schools in Dubuque.

In designing a learning expedition on astronomy, Rafael Hernandez fifth-grade teacher Eloise Biscoe said she and her colleague Wanda Muriel wanted to demystify the stars, solar system, and universe. They wanted to show students how seemingly remote and removed astronomical concepts actually figure into their everyday lives.

"It seemed important to reach them at that level first so they would know, 'Yes, it does affect my life in the most basic way: night, days, and seasons,'" Biscoe said. "Those are just basic things, but they exist because of the way the earth moves in space and how it is situated in its relation to the sun. And that's astronomy."

It's About Time

Since the concept of time carries through the entire expedition, Biscoe and Muriel call the learning expedition "It's about Time." Time is the connecting thread through three broad topics: the movements of the earth and the moon, the universe, with a focus on constellations, and the solar system. Students began learning about the earth's movements through a number of small projects, such as making sundials with a stick and a piece of paper to measure time.

"Starting with time and starting with something they could observe themselves really allowed them some sort of firsthand experience besides just looking up at the stars," said Biscoe, who has taught the expedition three years in a row.

Many of the discovery-oriented experiments the students conducted during the expedition were developed by Project Aries, an astronomy education project at the Center for Astrophysics at Harvard College Observatory in Cambridge. The experiments teach students about time using simple, inexpensive equipment that the students build themselves. A shoebox, ball, skewer or pencil, black spray paint, and a flashlight become the Astronomy Lab. The

> To apply what they were learning through the activities, Biscoe's students kept a "moon journal," recording each time they saw the moon, its location, and shape.

Lab gives students a visual grasp of why the earth is round, teaching the movement of the earth and the concepts of day and night and seasons by analyzing shadows.

To apply what they were learning through the activities, Biscoe's students kept a "moon journal," recording each time they saw the moon, its location, and shape. Discussions often focused around their journals. "I'd ask the kids what shape it was, where it was in the sky, where they saw it, and for predictions about what it would look like next," Biscoe said. "I cut out its shape and put it on a calendar, and they could see that it was growing or getting smaller."

After gaining an understanding of the earth and moon, the class visited the University of Massachusetts' observatory in Boston to observe stars and planets through a telescope.

Students reflected on such experiences in their "Astro Notebooks," a compilation of records of their experiments, structured thoughts on scientific readings, reflections, and predictions, with specific criteria for each type of entry.

As part of an investigation of the solar system, students researched vital statistics of one planet and drew a creature who could live on that planet and adapt to it.

"It was difficult for them to understand how you would adapt a body of a creature to live on a planet," Biscoe said. "They eventually understood that if it was a gaseous planet you would have to fly or swim through, or if it was very hot they would have tiny, pointy feet so they wouldn't have to stand on the planet."

To complement the science projects, Biscoe and Muriel integrated language arts into the expedition. Students read astronomy-related literature, such as a Kenyan fable and short stories. The historical fiction work *Willy Bea and the Time the Martians Landed* depicts the reactions of an Ohio farm family to the 1938 Orson Welles broadcast of *War of the Worlds*. After reading science fiction stories and discussing the genre, students wrote their own science fiction stories.

For the final project, small groups of students created bilingual astronomy board games designed to be fun and educational, such as a journey through the solar system, resembling Monopoly or Chutes and Ladders. Given more time, Biscoe said, she

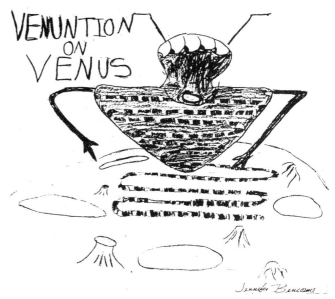

Venus has an atmosphere with only two gases, nitrogen and carbon dioxide. She will need to jump in order to breathe carbon dioxide. The temperature is more than 900 degrees Fahrenheit during the night and day. She would have to adapt with tough leathery skin so her insides won't burn up. The surface is really rocky. There are volcanoes and the floor is really hot. So in order to not get burned she would have to jump with her coiled body. Venuntion eats sulfuric acid that rains from the clouds on Venus.

Story and illustration by Jennifer Bencosme, a fifth grader at Rafael Hernandez School in Boston.

would have taught more minilessons on writing good directions and asked the students to design a mock-up game to play with other groups. Then they would give each other feedback.

The students were required to include twelve factual questions, but Biscoe said in retrospect that she thinks the groups could have done a better job of incorporating what they had learned about astronomy into the games. Next time, she said she might give them short quizzes or even a factual test. "One hopes they will know these things just through the experiments, but for me not enough of that happened."

Reach for the Stars

Journeys, like artists, are born not made. A thousand different circumstances contribute to them willed or determined by the will—whatever we may think. They flower spontaneously out of the demands of our natures—the best of them lead us not only outward in space, but inwards as well.

—Lawrence Durrell

Reference Books:
Burns, Marilyn. *This Book Is About Time.* Boston: Little, Brown, 1978.
Ranger Rick's Nature Scope: Astronomy Adventures 2:2 (1986).
Zubrowski, Bernie. *Clocks: Building and Experimenting with Model Timepieces.* New York: Beech Tree Books, 1988.

Fiction:
Hamilton, Virginia. *Willie Bea and the Time the Martians Landed.* New York: Macmillan, 1983.
Mollel, Tololwa M. *Orphan Boy.* New York: Clarion Books, 1990.

Newsletters/Magazines:
The Universe in the Classroom. Astronomical Society of the Pacific. Available free of charge to teachers, school librarians, and administrators. Write: Teachers Newsletter Dept., 900 Ashton Ave., San Francisco, CA 94112.

Sandra Drapeau, Steve Geisert, and Fran Kennedy preface the guide to the learning expedition "Reach for the Stars" with this allusion to space exploration and dedicate the expedition to "all who aspire to discover and marvel at the wonders of the universe."

The teachers use the metaphor of the journey in their plan:

"The course of this journey will not be an easy one, just as life's journey is not. It will be rigorous. It will be filled with challenges. These successes and failures will be deliberate to prepare travelers better for their own life journeys. At the end of this journey students will have a better view of the vastness of this universe and their role in it. One needs only to observe and reflect on the night sky to realize the richness and timelessness of it, and that we are one tiny particle in the total picture as we chart our life course."

While this might sound ethereal, these ideas are grounded in four guiding questions:

◆ What are the theories of the origin of the universe?
◆ Who are the pathfinders of astronomy, and what are their contributions?
◆ What are the celestial components of the universe?
◆ What are manmade objects in space?

In designing the learning expedition, Drapeau, Geisert, and Kennedy took the required sixth-grade astronomy curriculum and expanded it into a wide-ranging, discovery-oriented expedition that draws on

Videos:

Annie and the Stars of Many Colors. Fourth grade to middle school. A twenty-five-minute video that explores the life and work of astronomer Annie Jump Cannon.

So Many Galaxies, So Little Time. Junior high to adult. A forty-minute video about a team of scientists led by astrophysicists Margaret Geller and John Huchra who measure the red shifts of thousands of galaxies in an effort to map the large-scale structure of the universe.

Videos available from the Astronomical Society of the Pacific, $39.95. Tel.: (415) 337-2624.

their own passions and seeks to inspire their students. The expedition allows students to challenge themselves in a range of subject areas, including music, art, social studies, science, math, language arts, physical education, technology, and social skills.

"It's an integrated program where the kids are responsible for their own learning, and when they

◆ ◆ ◆

All the kids are able to do it. There's something for the brightest child and there's something for the child who is challenged by learning.

—Fran Kennedy

◆ ◆ ◆

are responsible for their learning and they take it seriously and they do well, they are proud of themselves," said Kennedy, who team teaches "Reach for the Stars" with Drapeau each spring semester. "All the kids are able to do it. There's something for the brightest child and there's something for the child who is challenged by learning."

After listening to *Space Songs*, poems by Myra Cohn Livingston, the students produce their own goals for the learning expedition by creating an astronomy chart listing what they know about astronomy, questions they have, and leaving blank a column labeled "answers we have found."

During the course of the expedition, students do a written or oral report on the origins of the universe, solve aerospace arithmetic problems, visit a local planetarium and make marshmallow constellations as part of their study of constellations, and meet in the evening with an amateur astronomer to identify constellations in the sky. Students also write a short report about a manmade space object or another topic in astronomy and practice presenting it orally. For an audience, the students give these reports as though it's a "wax museum." The students, frozen until an audience member pushes a "start button," come alive and deliver their reports.

As a service project in previous years, students have made alphabet books with astronomy themes, and organized a party for the day care center at a local hospital to read the books and play games, Kennedy said.

"What do they get from this? A feeling that they have contributed, that they have self-worth, that they matter in life, and they make a difference," Kennedy said.

Space Camp

Participating in Space Camp at the Challenger Learning Center in Des Moines completes the expedition for the students. Joe Dolan, a sixth-grade teacher at Table Mound Elementary in Dubuque, also teaches "Reach for the Stars." He said students prepare by learning geology and chemistry, and getting experience in team work. His group simulates a mission to the moon, each having a chance to work on the mission control and space station teams. Kennedy said that before attending Space Camp students must learn small and large group cooperation.

Students as Observers

As an offshoot of the "Reach for the Stars" expedition, Joe Dolan, a sixth-grade teacher at Table Mound Elementary in Dubuque, started an astronomy club. These students are connected via a modem line to the 24-inch refractor telescope at Mount Wilson Observatory near Los Angeles, which is open to educational groups across the country. Students work with an astronomer at Mount Wilson collecting data for one hour.

Using a software program called "The Sky," students research what the sky at Mount Wilson will look like on the night they are scheduled to observe. They are able to download the observations, and Dolan plans to create a catalogue of the observations over the years with information about each object. These will be shared with students working on the expedition. In the future, Dolan plans to gather images taken by scientists who have observed with the Hubble Space Telescope to compare with the Mount Wilson observations.

For information, write Telescopes in Education, P.O. Box 24, Mount Wilson, CA 91023, or call Gil Clark at (818) 395-7579.

Teacher Resources/Fieldwork:

Project Aries at the Center for Astrophysics at Harvard College Observatory in Cambridge, Massachusetts. For information, contact R. Bruce Ward at (617) 495-5434.

Getting Comfortable Teaching with Space, United States Space Foundation. Workshops for elementary and secondary teachers on integrating space information into the curriculum. For information, call (719) 550-1000.

For further resources, contact Expeditionary Learning school designer Marquita Jackson-Minot at (617) 576-1260, ext. 32.

I can give you all these ideas and tell you how I do it, but you have to want to do it, and it has to be your passion. That is very contagious to the students.

—Fran Kennedy

"They take the work seriously when we go to Space Camp," Kennedy said. "They know they have to be accountable, and so when they are accountable it becomes a part of them instead of just coming out of the book."

Although teachers who would like to do a learning expedition on astronomy can use the Dubuque guide or information gleaned from this article to help them design their own learning expedition, Kennedy said there are no recipes.

"I can give you all these ideas and tell you how I do it, but you have to want to do it, and it has to be your passion," she said. "That is very contagious to the students." All these things spark it, but your journey will be different from mine. The journey is never the same because the children are never the same." ◆

Amy Mednick is the editor of The Web.

From the Heart:

Songwriting Teaches Students about Communication, Selves

Mike Krapfl

Keshia Bridges stood silently, studying what she heard.

A big reel of tape turned through a fancy recording machine. Drums beat a rap rhythm through the speakers. Bridges' voice filled the recording studio with her own words ("I caught you creeping") about a cheating boyfriend.

"No," said the sixteen-year-old student from Dubuque's Central Alternative High School. "That doesn't sound right. The voice is too harsh," she said of her own work. "It needs to he softer."

"Okay," said Jim Berg, a musician and the recording engineer at Heartland Studios in Galena, Illinois. "Let's fix it."

And so they tried again.

That's life in a recording studio. There's always a judgment and a decision and—most likely—a revision to be made. It's difficult, painstaking work. But a small group of students from Central didn't seem to mind. These were their songs. They wanted to get them just right.

The twenty students milling about the recording studio on a recent weekday are taking a songwriting class at Central. They're getting English credits for their verses. And they're also getting the chance to plan, write, record, and sell a real album.

"You guys don't know how lucky you are to have a class like this," said Berg, who's donating his

November 20, 1994. *Telegraph Herald*. Published with permission of the *Telegraph Herald*.

Central High School students Melissa Gavin and Ardeth Fitz work with engineer Jim Berg on the recording of their song. Photograph by David Guralnick for the Telegraph Herald.

Jon Morrison, teachers Linda Smith and Dave Reel watch guitarist Cory Heim create music to match Reel's song. Photograph by David Guralnick for the Telegraph Herald.

time, the studio's time, and the time of some musician friends to the students' project.

The class is the work of Central teachers Linda Smith, who's written and recorded several albums of her own, and Dave Reel, who likes to sing along to a karaoke machine.

The songs were critiqued and revised. They were copyrighted. The students washed cars and otherwise tried to raise money to cover the $600 cost of putting their album on cassettes.

"We tried to make this as real-life as possible," Smith said of the class. The songs were critiqued and revised. They were copyrighted. The students washed cars and otherwise tried to raise money to cover the $600 cost of putting their album on cassettes.

And then they went to the recording studio.

Ardeth Fitz and Melissa Gavin, sixteen-year-old juniors, found a back room where they could rehearse their song. It's called "Daddy's Coming Home." It's about child abuse. It's not pretty: "Daddy's coming home/He's gonna break another bone/All the pain is locked inside/There's nowhere to run, nowhere to hide/But you're all alone."

Smith and Reel listened as Fitz sang and Gavin helped with the chorus. "That's good, really good," Reel told them. "That's touching my soul."

Just around a corner, Mark Heacock, a seventeen-year-old junior, was getting nervous about singing the love song he wrote. Even so, he had lots of good things to say about the songwriting class. "I think it's a good class," he said. "I love it. I never knew I could write music until I took this class."

David Olson, Central's principal, said the class is successful because its teachers have a passion for their subject. And the class, he said, is a good example of Expeditionary Learning.

Central is one of four Dubuque schools trying the school reform project. Expeditionary Learning, just like the songwriting class, emphasizes learning by doing, revising work until it's as good as it can be, and completing a project.

But what about academics?

Students are developing communication skills by writing, reading, and working together, Olson said.

They're also learning something about the bottom line by going about the business of recording and selling an album.

And they're learning something about themselves.

"For a kid to decide whether to write a country song or a rock song or whatever is a major decision," Olson said. "It reveals who the kid is in a major way. I see kids exploring themselves and who they are through these songs."

I see kids exploring themselves and who they are through these songs.

—David Olson

◆ ◆ ◆

Back at the recording studio, Bridges was thinking about her rap song. It wasn't perfect. But it was getting there.

"I never thought it could go this far," she said. "I'm real proud of myself."

And then she turned to her teachers, laughed, and said: "I'm going to be a star, and it's all because of my songwriting class." ◆

Mike Krapfl is a reporter with the Dubuque Telegraph Herald.

Daddy's Coming Home

By Ardeth Fitz and Melissa Gavin

*I saw a frightened child on the corner
Hiding the tears from the word
All the pain is kept inside
Laughter is shown on the outside
As the sun goes down and the moon comes up
Tears will start to fall
It's a living hell the way we're raised
There are no sunny days.*

*Chorus:
Daddy's coming home
He's gonna break another bone
All the pain is locked inside
There's nowhere to run, nowhere to hide
But you're all alone*

Daddy's coming home, Daddy's coming, coming home.

*You know there's monsters out there
People don't seem to care
You tell your children there's no such thing
But it's a living hell when you're stuck in a dream.*

(Repeat chorus)

*Ending line:
My conscience is clear with only one fear, Daddy will
appear.*

Breaking the Mold:
The Shape of Schools to Come

Joanna Richardson

Table Mound students take a close-up look at one of the aircraft on display at Dubuque Regional Airport for their K-6 expedition on flight and transportation. Photograph by Dale Stierman.

Dubuque, Iowa

From the distance, the fat, cartoonish outline of the C-130 several thousand feet up looks like a clumsy bird hurtling through the clouds. Blink, and you might lose sight of the image for a moment in the afternoon haze.

But down here on the ground, the young spectators lock their gaze on the dark blip—and don't let go. Tilting their heads back to extremes, they shade their eyes with one hand in mock salute. A few point up. Others sit on the ground, frozen in an open-mouthed "gee whiz" expression as they wait for some sign from the Navy plane.

One of the women who has accompanied these junior air-show enthusiasts to Dubuque Regional Airport stands planted on a grass strip near the runway. She lets out a long "ooooh" as her excited charges chatter over two faint objects that have just shot silently from the tail of the plane. They hover for a moment and then fall like ribbons through the sky.

"That must be them! Here they come!" the woman says in one long breath. In a few minutes, she thinks, the "Leapfrogs"—the Navy SEALs parachute team—will come plunging toward land.

A third grader shoots a quick glance in the chaperone's direction. "It's not them," the girl says matter-of-factly. "They're just sending that out to test the wind direction before they jump. The plane will come around again." The woman nods a few times, as if she should have known this.

The plane does loop back around, and the Leapfrogs do jump—right in front of the throngs of students who whoop almost loudly enough to drown out the sound of chutes whipping in the wind.

When the parachutists finally touch down, the children pummel them with questions about the life of a Leapfrog. Then it's off to check out the planes and helicopters on display around the concourse.

As they climb in and out of the cockpits, the youngsters can't resist the impulse to reach out and touch the larger-than-life machines. After all, for the past two weeks, they've written stories about them, learned how they're made, studied how they work, and read about all the places they go. So the eager students run their fingers over every inch of metal they can. Some even grab the controls, as if pulling hard enough might actually result in liftoff.

Because today, you see, the airport is their school. This is "Expeditionary Learning."

In theory, it sounds like a simple enough idea: Get children out of the classroom, let them take more control of their learning, give them lots of time to test their ideas and fuel their natural curiosity, and organize their studies around central themes that make school more exciting, challenging, and real.

November 9, 1994. Excerpted from *Education Week.* Reprinted with permission.

Not so radical, maybe. But in practice, the concept of Expeditionary Learning turns the old lecture-and-drill method of teaching inside out.

◆ ◆ ◆

Instead of learning in forty-minute fits and starts, the less structured school day lets students and teachers be more spontaneous and creative. In the process, its architects say, students also learn valuable lessons about life.

◆ ◆ ◆

Its proponents say the approach breaks down the walls between traditional academic subjects by weaving science, social studies, and English lessons into projects on everything from flight to publishing. Instead of learning in forty-minute fits and starts, the less structured school day lets students and teachers be more spontaneous and creative. In the process, its architects say, students also learn valuable lessons about life.

The school-based expeditions run about three to nine weeks and blend together several disciplines under a common theme. Students spend about 25 percent of their time out of the classroom—a big change from the periodic field trips of the past. The rest of their time is spent on hands-on classroom activities that require students to make connections between their studies and to draw their own conclusions.

Pieces of the curriculum are still taught in the traditional fashion. At Central High, for instance, many students take stand-alone reading and science courses in the afternoon. And the elementary schools usually offer math outside the time teachers set aside for expeditions.

Teachers also take care to make sure expeditions at every grade level meet the district's expectations for teaching such basic skills as reading, writing, and problem solving. But beyond that, schools design many activities simply to instill a love of books, the desire to learn, or the ability to work with others.

At Table Mound Elementary, for example, students of all ages worked for several weeks on units related to transportation, flight, and space exploration. Throughout such units, a variety of field trips brought their studies to life: demonstrations of hot-air balloons, a helicopter landing at the school, and, finally, a visit to the air show. In the end, some students took away new research, writing, and map-making skills.

Expeditionary Learning builds on the principles of Outward Bound, an outdoor-adventure program founded in England in 1941 by Kurt Hahn, an

King Middle School science teacher Tim Cronin and his student emerge from snorkeling, collecting specimens, and taking underwater photographs. Photograph by David Cornwell.

Jack Elementary School fifth-grade students Matt Lakin and Matt York draw illustrations for children's books on the ocean. Photograph by David Cornwell.

educator expelled from Nazi Germany. The program made its way to the United States in the 1960s, touting its wilderness expeditions as a way to teach about teamwork, leadership, and perseverance.

Outward Bound trips last up to three weeks and involve small groups in activities such as camping, rock climbing, and rope exercises. As the activities become increasingly difficult, participants learn to brainstorm on how to tackle problems together—an exercise that encourages both cooperation and self-reflection.

Now, Outward Bound proponents insist, students' expeditions like Table Mound Elementary's flight unit can help bring similar lessons to schools. By making learning more spontaneous and connecting it to the outside world, teachers can encourage students to discover that learning doesn't stop when the school bell rings.

In 1992 officials from Outward Bound and Expeditionary Learning Outward Bound U.S.A. its partner in Cambridge, Massachusetts, which oversees the project, competed with hundreds of other designers for a "break the mold schools" grant from the New American Schools Development Corporation. NASDC, a private, nonprofit corporation organized by business leaders during the Bush administration, is now providing funding to nine design teams—like Expeditionary Learning Outward Bound—carrying out their blueprints through 1995. After that, the teams will enter a two-year dissemination-and-replication period, when they are expected to require less outside support.

Four Dubuque schools have embraced Expeditionary Learning: Bryant, Lincoln, and Table Mound elementary schools, and Central High, an alternative school. Four "spirit schools" across the district have also adopted some features of the program, but the district—not the NASDC grant—is underwriting their projects.

In addition to Dubuque, seven other Expeditionary Learning schools are up and running in four cities across the country: Denver, Boston, New York, and Portland, Maine. Schools in San Antonio, Baltimore, and Decatur, Georgia, have also expressed interest in the approach, according to Expeditionary Learning officials.

The program's interdisciplinary curriculum is designed to make learning richer and to link it to everyday decisions. Teachers weave technology, for example, through most of the expeditions at every grade level. But other subjects aren't so easy to work in. Most teachers continue to present mathematics, which they say is the most difficult subject to integrate, in an isolated block.

"Traditionally in education, we have little pockets of learning—thirty minutes of this or forty minutes of that," says Nancy Bradley, the district's associate director of staff development. "And kids don't necessarily make that quantum leap from one isolated piece of learning to another. Now, I think they understand much more about how their learning connects to the real world and to other subjects they work on."

Kindergartners from the Rafael Hernandez School in Boston and their teacher Carmen Zaya collect ants at a nearby park as part of an expedition on insects. Photograph by David Cornwell.

Teachers also stress character development throughout the curriculum. "How to Launch a Dream," one of Table Mound Elementary's recent miniexpeditions, featured a model-rocket project and other hands-on activities to teach about the importance of setting—and attaining—personal goals.

But while schools want children to learn about both success and failure, Scott Gill, a school designer for the project, is quick to add that teachers must follow the rule of "guided discovery"—nudging students along in the right direction. "Sometimes, when we let kids fail in things that are significant, it ends up demoralizing them and knocking them down," he explains. "Then they're not likely to take risks again."

Throughout each expedition, students set aside time to reflect on their learning in daily journals. One entry in a fourth grader's journal written during Table Mound's flight expedition featured long descriptions about everything from the principles of flight to the history of the commercial airlines to the use of planes in World War II.

In keeping with the program's central features, teachers encourage students to share control over the curriculum. A learning experience is richer, the theory goes, when it includes personal challenge and an element of the unknown.

"Kids are, in some ways, just paddling along and letting others be the leaders," Gill explains, "But we've said, no, the concept of an expedition is jumping in. We have to let kids know, 'You have to pay attention because you're going to have to perform.'"

So teachers encourage students to make daily decisions about how to approach an expedition. In the fourth-grade flight expedition, for example, students were allowed to rank a list of theme-related activities, including visits from flight instructors in the community, a field trip to the aviation center for research, and a variety of social studies and science projects. Of course, this flexibility also means teachers often revise their plans for the next day based on their students' interests.

The district has also been matching teachers with students, a practice called "looping." For example, first-grade teachers follow their students to the second grade, but then loop back to pick up another first-grade class, starting the two-year process all over again. The aim is to build trust and a sense of community, an environment much like "the old country schoolhouse," says Superintendent Marvin O'Hare.

Even though they have the same teacher for more than one year, students don't repeat expeditions. Instead, each expedition is geared toward a specific grade level. Teachers can use these plans year after year, but they're expected to come up with new ones to add to the mix and share ideas from other sites.

The time and planning involved in writing the expeditions has been both a professional windfall and a tremendous strain for teachers. "You cannot diminish the importance of the teacher and the teacher buy-in to make this a success," Lesley Stephens, the principal of Bryant Elementary, says. "It's a tremendous load for teachers . . . the resources needed and the preparing for expeditions."

Teachers were trained to write Expeditionary Learning plans in the first and second years of the grant. Because an expedition can cross several disciplines, typically a group of teachers will come together to collaborate. But the writing process involves more than just coming up with interdisciplinary lessons and fun field trips.

Teachers must make sure each expedition meets the district's strict curriculum expectations in each subject area. District officials and a handful of national education organizations review the plans, Gill says. What's more, schools have also asked teachers to defend their ideas before their colleagues, parents, and community members.

Tammy Duehr, a second-grade teacher at Table Mound Elementary, admits the work has been stressful, but she says the payoffs are worth it. "That's a key part of this," she explains. "The teachers are really getting to create."

John Burgart, the district's associate director of instruction and the project director for Expeditionary Learning, says teachers seem to finally feel ownership of the curriculum. "For many years, we operated under the sort of "teacher proof" curriculum," he says with a hint of sarcasm. "Everything was packaged for them. Now, they really have to know the district's expectations and be a curriculum planner and developer."

Most of teachers' planning and writing time falls over the summer and in minisabbaticals and release days during the school year. But many still complain that they don't have enough daily planning time to keep up with their flexible classroom—and field trip—schedules.

On top of these in-service days, teachers and school officials juggle several other staff-development projects throughout the year, many of them sponsored by groups like Project Adventure or the Voyageur Outward Bound School in Minnesota, which are design-team partners for the national project. In fact, professional development—on everything from assessment training to river rafting—has been the biggest expense under the grant.

Orca, by Carlos Santiago, a fourth grader at the Rafael Hernandez Bilingual School in Boston, for the learning expedition "Marine Mammals: Into the Deep Blue Sea."

Of the $250,000 the district received for 1994-95, about $135,000 went toward staff-development purposes, including honoraria for teachers and pay for substitutes. Another chunk of funding has gone toward trips to help teachers write their expeditions. Last summer, for example, the district paid for a fifth- and sixth-grade teacher from Table Mound Elementary to travel to the U.S. Air Force Academy to learn about rocketry for an expedition on space travel.

The Expeditionary Learning approach has ushered in an "immediate, major menu of opportunities" for teachers, says Bradley, Dubuque's associate staff-development director. "You can imagine what a shift this is for teachers who used to beg just to drive to Des Moines for a conference."

Despite the extra time and training involved in adopting the new approach, Expeditionary Learning seems to be taking hold. It's gone over particularly well in the elementary schools where the day already has a fairly loose structure and teachers are accustomed to blending several subjects together in their lessons. And, elementary teachers say, keeping their options open has always made sense: sometimes they have to make a sudden change of course just to keep the children's attention.

But Expeditionary Learning seems trickier to pull off at the high school level. There, teachers tend to be less collaborative, and academic requirements place all sorts of restrictions on how the school day gets organized.

At Dubuque's Central High, an alternative school where about thirty-five of 170 students have severe learning disabilities, the staff was already accustomed to finding creative ways around the system. But the shift to Expeditionary Learning still left both teachers and administrators feeling overextended at times.

"It was so hard last year we weren't even sure we'd make it sometimes," confides David Olson, Central's principal. "We did everything at once. So there was no falling back because all the old ways were gone."

The school had to rearrange and open up blocks of time. The staff had to get comfortable with an interdisciplinary curriculum—a stretch for high school teachers accustomed to being "specialists." Teachers had to come up with new ways to teach a student body that has a tough time dealing with change. Some students are themselves parents, and many others are dropouts who had little success in more traditional schools.

But the school finally hit smoother waters this year, Olson says, and the staff members seem excited and more comfortable in their new environment. Now, the day is divided so students spend a block of time in the morning on their longer expeditions, which weave together two to three traditional subjects. In the afternoon, their schedule looks more like a conventional high school student's, although teachers continue to follow the principles of Expeditionary Learning.

Sue Schmuck, a physical education teacher, says the new approach helped her refine her teaching style. "It really pushed me to have a good grasp of what I'm teaching," she says. "And I think the kids really see me in a different light now: I wasn't just having fun in the gym."

But students are proving to be a tougher sell when it comes to Expeditionary Learning at Central High. Not only do the teenagers bring their own special circumstances to the alternative school, but like most students their age, the high schoolers are skeptical of anything a teacher claims will be "fun."

"Most kids will tell you they don't like Expeditionary Learning because it's more work," Principal Olson points out. "Our expectations for their learning are higher. With all the changes, the kids can't just slide by."

Jeremiah, who's come down to the river to do some fishing for his "Metric Sports" class, agrees. "Central used to be a slacker school," he says, keeping a close eye on his line. "It keeps getting harder and harder. But you learn more instead of sitting in class all day, which is what would make people want to drop out."

Overhead, a train idles on the old railroad bridge that will carry it to Wisconsin or Illinois just across the Mississippi River. A couple of girls from the class sit and talk on a rock ledge while their classmates measure and weigh their catches or wait patiently to hook a fish. Metric Sports, a physical education course with a twist, is designed to teach students the practical applications of metrics through physical outings like this fishing expedition.

Tim Ebeling, one of the teachers who's brought the class here, takes the girls' obvious lack of interest in stride. "Some of the kids, when you get on their case about it, you lose them the next time" [there's an activity], he explains. "We say Expeditionary Learning is challenge by choice."

Still, some students just don't know what to make of the new ways. The fieldwork "just doesn't make sense to me," admits Ian, a burly student whose glasses and fuzzy beard make him appear older than he is. "We're more likely to smoke and goof off when we're out of school" for a project, he adds defiantly.

But with time, Central administrators say students have come to appreciate—and even enjoy—the new approach to learning. Karol Cervantes, an eighteen-year-old Central graduate who now waits tables at Chi Chi's Mexican restaurant while attending community college in nearby Peosta, says the emphasis on self-discovery brought her closer to her teachers, though she admits things were difficult at times.

"The first semester, everyone was new at it," she says of the 1993-94 school year. "We barely had a clue what we were doing, and the teachers hardly had a clue. I had a hard time getting adjusted, and some of my friends dropped out because of the changes. But they went back this year."

"More and more kids want to be at Central now," Olson says, "instead of looking at this as their last option for education." For proof, the principal points to the school's waiting list of a dozen students.

◆ ◆ ◆

One program feature that helped win over students at Central is service learning. What's more, the practical work experience also seems to go over well with parents, who say they hope their teenagers will have a better shot at finding a job after graduation.

Unfortunately, administrators say the service learning component of the program has been hard to integrate. Sometimes, Gill admits, teachers have "had to contrive some things to get it in." At Central, for example, students help out at area businesses under a program that has no clear connection to their expeditions. But district officials say they've brought in consultants to help schools improve and expand on the service learning connections.

About a dozen Central students get credits for spending their mornings pitching in around the community under the "City as School" program. Most go where their interests lie, working at the local parks department, for example, or the community-access television station.

Wendy Miller, a business teacher and a coordinator of the project, says the exposure to the work-

place "has made the kids realize they can do more than they think they can. They always wanted to know, 'What's in it for me?' Now, we're starting to seek kids more willing to give of themselves."

Miller and Olson say they've watched students who were once indifferent to school—where learning meant cracking books all day and turning in worksheets—finally become interested in something.

Robert, a lanky sixteen-year-old from Central, is doing a five-week rotation at The Farmacy, a

◆ ◆ ◆

"Kids are, in some ways, just paddling along and letting others be the leaders. But we've said, no, the concept of an expedition is jumping in. We have to let kids know, 'You have to pay attention because you're going to have to perform.'"

—Scott Gill,
Dubuque Community Schools

◆ ◆ ◆

veterinarian's office and pet store downtown. He learned how to care for animals on the farm where he was raised, but he says he wants to find out more about the field. Robert does everything from prepping the animals for procedures to actually observing or assisting in surgery—an experience that made him a little woozy on the first and second go-round.

His friend Jason, who's come to meet him at the vet's office so they can head back to Central for the afternoon, works around the corner at Prescott Elementary School. An affable but intense fifteen-year-old, Jason says he has already singled out a handful of children there who he thinks may be headed for the same troubles he's had: a lack of

Students Cody Hearn and Anthony Lindemann, of Table Mound Elementary School in Dubuque, take measurements of their sand castle designed and constructed during an architecture expedition. Photograph by David Guralnick.

focus in school and a tendency to act out. He's excited about trying to take them under his wing. He's started a basketball group and talks frequently with the school's social worker about other ways to get through to the children.

District officials have no clear indication yet that Expeditionary Learning is boosting student achievement, Superintendent O'Hare admits. He says officials still need to evaluate all of the reforms under way in schools to see if they're making a difference. In the meantime, the education school at the University of Colorado at Boulder and the Academy for Educational Development have also been evaluating the district's progress, and the Rand Corporation is reviewing all of the NASDC sites.

Though test scores are up overall in Dubuque, it's hard to pinpoint which, if any, of the district's initiatives is the cause, Gill says. (And children in Iowa already do well in national test comparisons, he adds, typically scoring in the eightieth to ninetieth percentile.)

But at some of the Expeditionary Learning schools, subtle signs of improvement do indicate that the approach is making inroads. Principal Kathryn Kolarich of Lincoln Elementary says her students have become more motivated and more interested in the insights of their peers. And the school environment is more welcoming to parents—a change that has nearly doubled the number of parent volunteers on the school's roster, she says. Officials at the other schools say improvement in student attendance may also mean that the changes are catching on with students.

O'Hare points to an even more striking improvement: how the approach has reinvigorated teachers and principals. "The beauty of what's happening is that it's changing our people," he says, "That's the heart of the whole thing."

And if they see more signs of its benefits, school officials say, they hope Expeditionary Learning will catch on in more schools here. But they're not pushing it. The district doesn't want to force the approach on anybody, Burgart, the Expeditionary Learning project director, adds. For the time being, officials are content to focus on a handful of schools, where Expeditionary Learning is still evolving.

"One piece of this I sort of underestimated is the energy it takes to work with the staff, the parents, and the community to help them understand" [what the district is doing], adds Principal Stephens from Bryant Elementary. "The fieldwork's the frosting on the cake. But we still have to get across that the basics are really still there and kids are going to be able to compete." ◆

Joanna Richardson is a former Education Week *staff writer who now lives in Melbourne, Australia.*

Designing Fountains:
Making Quadratic Equations Come Alive

Angela Mattison, with Phil Gonring

Shy and tentative, two of my sophomore math students approached me one afternoon in early fall with their designs for a fountain. One idea was of a snub-nosed dolphin with water spraying out of its mouth. The other portrayed a couple of green students throwing up their lunch at a precise 30-degree angle. Realizing that teenagers could be inspired by adolescent humor, I did not want to squelch their enthusiasm.

"Do something fun; make it exciting," I said. Answering my challenge, they set about drawing side and aerial views of their elaborate creation, deriving its equation and making graphs. As part of a mathematics learning expedition on fountains, they visited parks to view fountains in the community, and wrote a story, excerpted here, about the origin of their fountain:

Our fountain is called "The Fountain of Spewth." It represents the school's lunches and stands as a memorial to all children who have no choice but to eat the cafeteria food. If it were constructed, we would place it in the cafeteria for the children to sit around and use—if necessary! We would construct it of cement and there would be puke-green lights in the statues' mouths and in the pool to cast a sea-green tint over the water.

Other students took more classical approaches. One student designed the "Fountain of the Rising Sun," with its large diamond-shaped reflecting pool decorated as a compass with alternating mirror and blue tiles. He described the front view for his audience:

The view from the front would be three mountains, two seven-feet tall and one ten-feet tall. Extending from the tallest mountain there is a sun that is made of gold. The two arcs would cross over the sun. The stream from the right or "east" side would cross just in front of the sun, the stream on the left or "west" side of the fountain would cross behind the sun. On the tallest mountain there is a stream of water trailing down the slope, and when there is 2½-feet left until the stream hits water level, it drops off a waterfall into the reflecting pool. All of this will be lit up by lights at each of the four corners of the diamond. The lights are one foot under the water and shining up at the sun. Having these lights under water would not just light up the mountains, but they would light up the water also.

When the students completed their learning expedition, they displayed a wide range of fountain designs, based on quadratic equations, at an exhibition of student work for parents and other members of the community. Their drawings, computations, graphs, journal writings, and stories provided the focal point of a lot of discussion and laughter. The class also designed and built a group fountain. Framed by a wooden railroad-tie box, the pump inside emitted a mushroom spray, which the students had decided would be soothing and would sound appropriate for the school. The learning expedition impressed skeptics and friends because of the solid, meaningful math work, as well as the fact that the students integrated into the project other disciplines, both art and writing.

The night of the presentation of the designs marked a moment of personal growth for me as well. I was impressed with myself because I had lived up to a promise I made earlier in the year to move out of the comfort zone of traditional mathematics instruction. I had managed to step away from the chalkboard and give my students an opportunity to learn a concept in depth and apply it to something real: a fountain.

This movement away from convention began when my colleagues and I met to plan expeditions during the summer of 1995. At that time, I decided to pilot an idea by doing an expedition suggested in my textbook (McDougal/Littell, *Integrated 2 Mathematics,* Boston: Houghton Mifflin, 1995). I knew I had to teach my students quadratic equations and factoring—abstract concepts that many have difficulty grasping—and that the text called for a unit project to design a fountain. I decided to plan an expedition based on this idea, but I needed to make our study more than just a thematic unit by adding

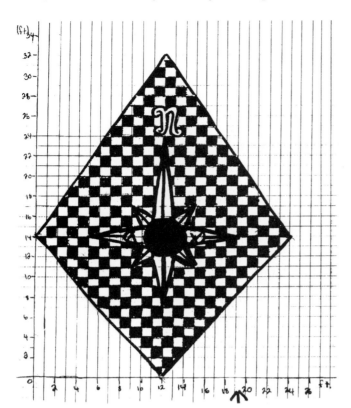

Aerial view of Fountain of the Rising Sun by high-school student Charles Boynton, of the Rocky Mountain School of Expeditionary Learning in Denver, reveals a pool decorated with a diamond-shaped compass.

key components of an expedition: integrated disciplines, fieldwork, individual and group work, expert instruction, and projects, which would provide my students with discovery-based, authentic experience. I was going to teach math in a way I had not been taught.

In planning the expedition, I included four major instructional objectives suggested by our school's standards: to teach students how to

◆ graph quadratic equations
◆ solve quadratic equations by factoring and/or by using the quadratic formula
◆ solve quadratic equations involving complex numbers
◆ solve systems of quadratic equations

I thought that the fountain unit would allow me to teach the content in an expeditionary way and still meet my instructional objectives. In the past, I had been frustrated by my participation in interdisciplinary expeditions that did not allow me to meet my instructional goals. When I first came to the school, I remember sitting down with my teammates to plan the year's first—and my first—expedition for students

in grades seven through ten. We chose a theme, *Las Montañas*, the mountains, and planned a week-long adventure trip that would take our students to the summit of a 14,000-foot peak, Mount Massive, and would involve rock climbing at Camp Hale. The humanities teachers gathered materials for the study of Colorado mining history and Romantic literature on nature. The science teacher prepared his students to mine for gold, and I prepared to teach geometric shapes, surface area, and volume. Excited by the potential of Expeditionary Learning, we prepared for the total integration of curriculum. We were naive.

Soon after starting the expedition, I found my students lacked interest because they had learned the content in the fifth grade. I actually wasted eight weeks of my students' time covering surface area and volume. "If we were at our old schools, we'd be doing algebra, not fifth- and sixth-grade work," my students complained. It took me a couple more expeditions and some hard lessons, but eventually I understood that when my team planned an expedition I needed to make sure that the math content would meet the standards for the students' grade levels. I couldn't always teach probability and statistics or measurement just to "fit" into my team's expeditions.

◆ ◆ ◆

> I had managed to step away from the chalkboard and give my students an opportunity to learn a concept in depth and apply it to something real: a fountain.

◆ ◆ ◆

As a result of my frustrations, I set out on my own and planned a self-contained expedition to address both the math standards and the demands of Expeditionary Learning. I allowed the textbook to serve as an outline for my expedition. The text suggested that the final individual project include a sketch of a fountain involving the height and width of the water arc, graphs of the arc along with their equations, the angles, and the water speed. I raised the stakes and made the unit more integrated and authentic by requiring journal writings; a story about the fountain; the calculations for finding the speed of the water arcs and for figuring out the quadratic equation for the parabola formed by the water arc; and expert instruction by a local fountain builder. And then, finally, I decided that the class as a whole would construct a fountain for the school.

This decision did not come easily. I agonized over whether or not my students should build a fountain for weeks. I was so hesitant because I feared losing all the time I knew the construction would take. After all, I had to get my juniors ready for graduation.

But I was also afraid of failing. What if I decided to undertake this huge task and it bombed? Questions and concerns took hold of my mind: Where would I get the materials? Are the students going to want to do this? How am I going to get someone to help? Do I have time to worry about construction as well as instruction?

In the midst of all this anxiety, I decided to build the fountain. I took the step, and when you do right, good things happen. Almost immediately, our art coordinator, Jane Page, came to me and asked if she could help in any way. It turned out Jane had a number of resources in the art community and even knew of some artists who had built fountains around Denver. She created a list of fountains in the city where I could take my students. Jane also recalled that she had taken a class on building fountains and gave me the name and number of the instructor who could answer my questions on how to build a fountain.

This man not only taught classes on how to build fountains, but also owned his own water landscaping business. He visited the school and talked to me about what it would take to pull this off. Excited to see hands-on learning taking place in our school, he encouraged me to build the fountain. The conversation eased my mind. At one point, he even said, "You should be very proud of yourself. The fact that you are even attempting this is great, and I will definitely help make sure that the actual building of the fountain will happen if that is what you really want."

So my concerns about how to construct the fountain, who would help, and where to get the material were eased. The air finally escaped from my lungs. The expert agreed to donate a number of the materials, and the rest of the supplies, such as the wood and the pump, students collected by making phone calls to lumber yards and hardware stores. As a result, we received free labor, consultation, and materials.

For four weeks I instructed my students in the basics of the mathematics of quadratic equations. Every one of my students had seen a fountain—either out in the field, in a book, on television, on slides in art class, or at the mall. In fact, I also required them to seek out and further examine fountains in the Denver area. This allowed them to see mathematics modeled in the real world, to see quadratic equations in an arc of water. As a result

As a result of the prior experience and their fieldwork, all the students could visualize a water arc.

of the prior experience and their fieldwork, all the students could visualize a water arc. Each time I taught a concept about quadratic equations, I could apply that concept to their image of a water arc.

As students picked up the concepts, they became anxious to get started on their fountain designs. They had some questions to answer: What did they want the angle of their water arc to be? Its height? Distance? Did they want the arcs to intersect?

The students then used their selected angles, heights, and distances of the arcs to calculate the speed. They used the following formula for their calculations:

$$y = \frac{-16 \, x^2}{v^2 \cos^2 a} + x \tan a$$

where a equals the angle at which the water leaves the starting point; v equals the velocity of the water; x equals the horizontal distance the water arc travels; and y equals the vertical distance that the water arc travels.

Given what they learned in four weeks of instruction on quadratic equations, they set out to derive the equations and graphs for the paths of their water arcs—a lengthy process. First, students had to decide at what angles their water would leave the ground, how high the water would spray in the air, and how far the water would travel. Once they had

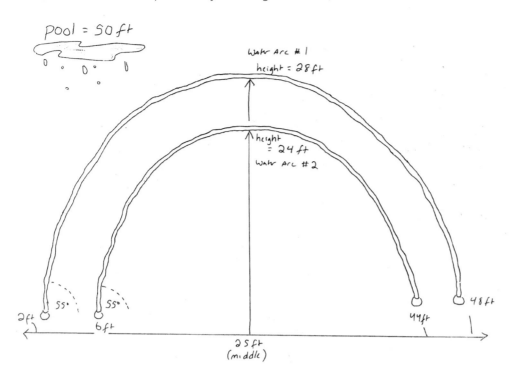

pool = 50 ft

Water Arc #1
height = 28 ft

↑ height = 24 ft
Water Arc #2

55°   55°

2 ft   6 ft   44 ft   48 ft

25 ft
(middle)

Fountain design by Lisa Bay and Tania Del Rio, sophomores at Rocky Mountain School of Expeditionary Learning in Denver, for a mathematics learning expedition on designing fountains.

made these choices, they calculated the speed using the above equation, and drew initial graphs of the water arcs' paths. They later verified that the graphs were correct after they derived the equation for the water arc. To derive the equation, they used what they knew about quadratic equations and the factored form. By plugging their information into the factored form $a(x - p)(x - q)$, where p and q are the points at which the water arc leaves and lands, and calculating it to get it in the standard quadratic form $ax^2 + bx + c$, they derived the equation of their water arcs. They could then check their answers by plugging in points to see if their graphs were correct, and actually modeled their equation.

While students worked on their individual fountain designs, the class constructed its own fountain. Instead of trying to build one of the student's individual designs, we decided to brainstorm more simplistic models to build. After all, this was my first time building a fountain. The fountain builder came in and spent an entire class period with my students. He broke them into small groups to brainstorm ideas for fountains. In their groups they decided what the reflecting pool would be made of, its shape, and the appearance of the centerpiece. They also came up with ideas for where to get the materials. Back in a large group, the class reached a consensus on the construction of a square wooden reflecting pool with the school logo, cut from sheet metal, as the cen-

terpiece. The students agreed that they would seek donations of material.

The entire process took longer than I had planned. I had allotted six weeks, but it took eight or nine. Nevertheless, I felt the expedition was successful for a number of reasons, not all academic. To pull off the fountain expedition, I had to step outside my circle. I found my students going beyond their preconceived limits as well.

Candy, a fifteen-year-old professional model with manicured fingernails and a hundred-dollar smile, stepped out of her comfort zone by leading the fountain construction crew and spending two days sawing and hammering spikes into redwood, getting slivers in and dirt on her hands.

Another girl, a quiet, unobtrusive artist of fifteen, complained (through a friend of course) that she didn't want to make the calls to find donors for the wood. I didn't have to ask her friend about her reluctance as I pictured her on the phone, her voice, timid and barely audible, whispering, "This is the Rocky Mountain School of Expeditionary Learning. Can we have some wood? No? Okay . . . Good-bye." Yet she went ahead and did it, jumping out of her circle. In fact, she acquired a lot of wood—enough to make the class fountain, with some left over.

Still another girl worried about her initial plans to include a nude in her fountain design, especially because she knew our school enrolled first graders as well as eleventh graders. After discussions with the class and with Phil about censorship and the artistic value of her fountain design, she decided to go ahead with her initial plan.

These young women and their classmates then displayed the class fountain and their individual projects at the exhibition night. After hearing for a year from students and parents that the math program wasn't challenging or expeditionary enough, I was glad to see the high quality of work that was produced when students were challenged and when the learning was constructed in an interdisciplinary, hands-on, authentic, and expeditionary way. I was also pleasantly surprised by how well some of the students who most often didn't do well had performed. My students displayed fountains incorporating Godzilla, a fairy, a nude, the school logo, and Fruitopia bottles. The calculations were correct, the graphs accurate, and the art pleasing to the eye. I knew my students had learned a great deal.

I had learned a great deal too. I had a better grasp of what it means to teach math in an expeditionary school. I had a better understanding of how to integrate content in expeditions and the degree to which students should uncover, as opposed to cover, curriculum. In other words, I better understood how much time I should spend at the chalkboard covering material and how much time I should spend allowing my students to uncover material in discovery-based lessons.

But the process of reaching those conclusions evolved over time. When RMSEL first opened, the staff took Expeditionary Learning's charge to develop interdisciplinary curriculum to an extreme. Teams of teachers tried to integrate every single discipline in every theme. Teachers incorporated quantitative reasoning, cultural understanding, communication, art, science, and so forth, within the context of expeditions on the 1960s, the rain forest, community, and the judicial system. It was easy to think in these idealistic terms, since RMSEL didn't have a Regents exam, district-mandated curriculum, or outcomes dictated by a school board looming over its head. The staff developed the school's own standards and curriculum, which gave the teachers flexibility in designing interdisciplinary expeditions.

I joined RMSEL's staff the second year of the school's existence, fell into the "integrate at all costs" trap, and wrote curriculum like the *Las Montañas* expedition described earlier. When you fall into that trap the expedition can often lose its integrity. For instance, one of my colleagues now

laughs as he thinks about teaching about gang violence within the context of an expedition on the mountains and calling this brand of youth violence "a mountainous social issue." It's a lot like what my colleagues say happened the first year when they entitled their expedition on the 1960s "Culture, Conflict, and *Ciencia*," as if this sound bite implied that the teachers were going to teach science in Spanish.

Questions and concerns took hold of my mind: Are the students going to want to do this? Do I have time to worry about construction as well as instruction?

As the math teacher, I got out of this trap in planning my third expedition. Potential themes for this expedition included "the hospital," "hunger," and "the Maya." I recall my teammates' excitement: "Oh, yeah, Angela, you can calculate the stats on hunger in certain populations, or in certain areas" and "You can find the surface area of the biodome," and even "You can find the probability for survival of a patient who is admitted suffering from a certain form of cancer." One colleague even suggested that I teach my students Mayan math. While I wanted to help him out, I didn't want to spend weeks doing dots and lines, the basis of Mayan math, because I didn't want to neglect my students' needs to cover more of the required content.

I told my colleagues that I could not continually teach probability, statistics, and measurement as I had in the past. After all, students have to take SATs, graduate, and meet state requirements—of which Mayan math is not one.

A real dilemma is the catch-22 position my colleagues and I are placed in. Even though we had flexibility in the creation of our standards, colleges, universities, states, and districts demand that an enormous amount of content be covered in the course of the high school years. In other words, colleges and universities seem to dictate to the math teacher that she must be the source of all knowledge and demand rote memorization of theorems, postulates, and equations. This requirement flies in the face of good teaching theory, which suggests that learning is at its best when a student constructs her own knowledge. Allowing students to confront real problems, like the construction of a fountain, and then letting them play with the mathematics necessary to build it does not easily fall into line with the scope and sequence of conventional high school courses that takes students from algebra and geometry to calculus. Constructing knowledge takes much more time than imparting it, so it is only natural that teachers believe they don't have time to do integrated teaching. In fact, this concern created anxiety when I thought about building the fountain.

My real struggle as a teacher has been to try to work through this dilemma and find a balance. I know I can't integrate math in all expeditions; if I did, students wouldn't learn the content they need. I know I can't allow students the time to uncover curriculum as they did during the fountain expedition because high school would last seven years. So what do I do?

It's important to find a balance between integrating the math into an interdisciplinary expedition, and teaching skill and content work out of the context of an expedition. There is no way for students to explore every concept in depth and apply the learning to real life and still cover all the content required to graduate in four years of high school. Therefore, I have to decide which content is best explored in discovery-based applications and which just has to be covered as quickly as possible.

Right now, I am starting a new solo expedition with a group of eighth and ninth graders. They are going to design a skate park and learn about direct variation, trigonometry, and slopes in the process. This expedition, like the fountain expedition, is a lot of hard work and has created some anxiety—but I have found that in the long run, it will pay off. For me, a newcomer to Expeditionary Learning, to continue to design solos like the fountain and skate expeditions, is to continue to step outside my circle. I hope to drag a few of my students with me. ◆

Angela Mattison is a math teacher at the Rocky Mountain School of Expeditionary Learning in Denver. Phil Gonring is a former lead team member at RMSEL.

Natural Reflections

Katherine V. Stevens

Cal Follman sat down on the picnic table. His friends gathered around for the jokes, but there were none that day. He began to sketch, and one by one the boys slipped away to begin their own work, until there were only three tall, gangly boys sitting on the table intently focused on the old oak.

Cal was the best artist in the class, and his drawings of branches and leaf development were held up as models by his peers. Today we were in the park sketching trees. Soon students would be sketching their tree on Central High School's hillside to complete their learning expedition. This was practice, but for Cal it was more. In reflection and art he excelled. He need not be the clown in order to lead. Today, everyone's sketches were better. The idea of a tree and its personality was beginning to make sense.

The usual rendering of a trunk, with squirrel hole and cloudlike leaves and branches, was being replaced by torturous labor. Students were really seeing, really trying to make the vision before them come alive on the page. The time for light and shadow would come, but for now, the branches were not ruler straight, the leaves matched the tree identification, and the trunks were not opposing semicircular curves.

"Natural Reflections" is one of the strongest expeditions I teach, and perhaps the truest. In "Natural Reflections," for almost every student nature comes alive. They all think I am crazy at first, making each of them study and draw the development of one tree, although they all enjoy the daily walks around town to parks and the ice harbor. They remember the cloud formations, and how the daily temperature changed from March to June. Their journal reflections become less stilted and more

exact as they learn to focus on one natural item and use it as a basis for their daily entry. They also balk at the five required night entries; my students do not believe in homework.

Yet, the night entries are often their best, because the night is different, and many of them are creatures of the night—roaming to avoid home. As we all know, nature is a great healer. Some students begin with outright rebellion and refusal, manipu-

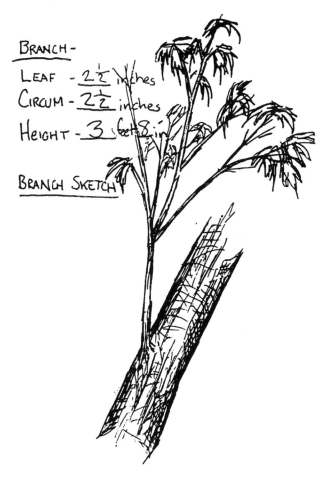

Artwork by Cal Follman, a student at Central Alternative High School in Dubuque, Iowa.

lating the hillside freedom to avoid work, yet even for these students nature wins.

Another day Jason Anderson climbed to the top of the bluff to escape from school. The bluff was almost straight up, layered with sandstone outcroppings and overgrown with brush. Students who chose trees midway up the hill slid on their way back down or ended in a dead run to keep their footing. Jason did not care. He was going to walk around on the top of the bluff, have a cigarette, and not worry about the assignment. But then he found the tree. And he kept going back to it.

I never did climb the hill, so I never did see the tree. But Jason's drawings and journals got better. He would write about lying on his stomach across the large rock and wondering how this tiny tree, only twenty-one inches tall—he measured it twice— could grow out of this rock.

Their journal reflections become less stilted and more exact as they learn to focus on one natural item and use it as a basis for their daily entry.

◆ ◆ ◆

He never did understand the part about the porosity of sandstone and the tenacity of root systems, but the last thing he did before he moved back home to

Artwork by Cal Follman, a student at Central Alternative High School in Dubuque, Iowa, for the "Natural Reflections" learning expedition.

Davenport was to climb the bluff with two friends to show them his tree. ◆

Katherine V. Stevens teaches English at Central Alternative High School in Dubuque, Iowa.

Part Two

Highlighting Character Development

We are part of the crew that works together. We are made strong by doing good deeds for others. One of the school's main jobs is to prepare students with the ability to learn from and help others.

—Chelsea Hester, fourth grade

Rocky Mountain School of Expeditionary Learning

Denver

Joining Intellectual and Character Development:

An Impossible Task?

Leah Rugen

Whenever we begin a project, it's an impossible task. I always want my students to feel that it can't be done. And then, somehow, we do it." That is how fourth-grade teacher Steven Levy recently described his approach to starting a new project with his students.

In many ways, planning a conference on character was an impossible task. The topic is vast and politically charged. But we felt a strong responsibility and need to organize a forum in which teachers might focus explicitly on a critical part of our design. After all, our original proposal states: "A dominant feature of our proposed New American School is an ethos where character development as well as universal intellectual achievement are viewed as the central mission of the school community."

At the two-day conference Joining Intellectual and Character Development, held at the Rocky Mountain School of Expeditionary Learning (RMSEL) in Denver, there was no hesitation among the sixty teachers who gathered to plunge into the topic and approach it from a variety of perspectives. We left with no simple answers or stepwise formulas, but began a rich exchange of insights, questions, and strategies.

Levy provided a valuable framework: "The question is not whether or not we can or should teach character. We are teaching character and values all

Mural design by Rocky Mountain School of Expeditionary Learning ninth-grade student Tania Del Rio. The large, colorful mural, which students helped trace and paint, was displayed at a mall nearby the school.

day, every day. Every decision we make, every judgment we administer, every interaction with every child demonstrates what we consider important in life, and serves as a model for our students about what really counts."

Daily Practice

A recurring theme of the conference was that character is a lens through which we should view everything we do.

"It's something I find myself working on every day, every hour," said Denver teacher Crystal Punch, in a panel discussion. She went on to describe the way in which questions of character permeate the daily routine of her class. "In my classroom I have a daily opportunity to talk about character, probably more than I care to, because the kids are always coming into situations where we have to stop and ask why that happened," she said. "We talk about the classroom and our responsibility for it. I put as much responsibility back onto them as I can."

◆ ◆ ◆

We left with no simple answers or stepwise formulas, but began a rich exchange of insights, questions, and strategies.

◆ ◆ ◆

Punch decided that her students needed more opportunities to notice and comment on each other's positive contributions to the classroom community. She initiated a practice in which every day different students acknowledged others for positive acts. On the first day, she thought they would begin with two students' acknowledgments. But when she asked for volunteers, she was amazed when seventeen hands went up. Everyone in the class wanted to say something positive about someone else. "It kept going on and on," Punch said. "At the end I was crying. I didn't think they saw that many nice things about each other."

The daily habit of reflection, explicit attention to constructive critique, and rituals such as morning

meetings are some of the ways in which character is built through practice.

"Character is not something that can be learned like geography or science," Levy said. "It has more to do with habits built over a long period of time. Habits are formed through repeated and continuous practice."

Physical Expression

It is important to remember that character is visible only through concrete actions. In a lunchtime talk, Greg Farrell, president of Expeditionary Learning, noted that Kurt Hahn, Outward Bound's founder,

Students James Denavit and Justin Daly take on the challenge of Rocky Mountain School of Expeditionary Learning's ropes course. Photograph by David Cornwell.

recognized that challenging physical activity engages character by "training the will for mastery." At Hahn's school, Gordonstoun, students developed individual training plans and set goals for their progress in physical activities. Each student competed with himself and his own self-perceived limits, rather than against others, through the discipline of daily physical exercise.

Moments of self-discovery and insight arise when people tackle physical challenges they feel are beyond them. "The body can teach you things that the mind will talk you out of," Farrell said. Someone making her way up a rock face for the first time realizes that she is capable of greater agility and strength than she thought was possible. Perhaps she is also capable of moving beyond other perceived limits.

◆ ◆ ◆

Moments of self-discovery and insight arise when people tackle physical challenges they feel are beyond them.

◆ ◆ ◆

Physical activity and action is most tied to character when it moves beyond the individual's experience to contribute to a greater good. Kurt Hahn's students served the community in many ways, including search and rescue activities along the coast of Scotland.

Service learning can prepare students to contribute in tangible ways. "Citizens are those who see problems and then do something about them," said Jim Toole of the National Youth Leadership Council, in a presentation at the conference. Toole noted that often children are the best citizens. When shown a complex social problem, a group of adults might throw up their hands. A class of fifth graders will ask, "What can we do?"

Connection to the Intellect

Service learning provides insight into what it means to join intellectual and character development as

The Chicks

Drawn by Grady Ryther

Drawing of chicks by first-grade student Grady Ryther for the "Living Things" expedition at the Rafael Hernandez School in Boston.

does the curriculum of Facing History and Ourselves, another focus of our conference. Toole commented that the goal of education should be "the application of knowledge for humane purposes." Students involved in acts of consequential service to the community, which they have chosen and developed, must draw upon their intellect and their character in solving real problems. Facing History and Ourselves, by using a case study approach to learning about the Holocaust, ignites personal emotions and values as well as critical thought.

By itself, the content and focus of students' learning is not enough to draw together character and intellect. What's needed is the "impossible task." In Levy's class, the children spent the year learning all about the bicycle and the history of the Lexington,

Dubuque parents write and share reflections on the Expeditionary Learning design principles. Photograph by Scott Gill.

Massachusetts, bike trail. One impossible task required that the fourth graders learn the necessary skills to repair seventeen bicycles in an in-class bike shop. After repair, the bikes were donated to other children who needed them. By the end of the year,

Character is not something that can be learned like geography or science. It has more to do with habits built over a long period of time.

—Steven Levy

◆ ◆ ◆

the children had also published a book called *On the Path*, a public resource about bicycles and the Lexington bike trail.

Such tasks do not grow out of fragmented curricula that are divided into bite-sized chunks. The best learning expeditions are built around impossible tasks that are achieved by the collective efforts of a community of learners.

The Individual and the Group

All learning requires a rich interplay between the individual and the group. Every learner needs time and opportunity to discover her own strengths and passions. A teacher mediates this process of self-discovery by creating a learning environment in which there are multiple paths to knowledge, time for solitude and reflection, and affirmation of diversity. Nurturing the individual child prepares the way for setting community goals for character.

"Character is developed through community and measured through acts that affect that community," said Phil Gonring, Denver lead teacher, in a panel discussion. How community is defined and which acts are valued is a complex matter. Schools and teachers who are able to avoid damaging conflict over issues of character and values seem to be those who reach out and involve parents and other community members. Developing goals for character with students and parents empowers them to take responsibility for learning.

Angela Cook of Paige Academy in Roxbury, Massachusetts, galvanized conference participants when she spoke of parent involvement at her school. "We have a mandatory meeting with parents every month. Everyone comes, and we discuss with them what we are planning to teach the children. For example, if we are going to talk about biases, we'll have a discussion with the whole parent group and the teachers. We are working together collectively."

Such forums create opportunities for parents to make meaningful contributions to the community. Differences become strengths rather than harmful divisions. We get into trouble only when we see the needs of the individual as separate and isolated from the needs of the community.

Farrell noted that it is a strange and wonderful paradox that personal passion always arises out of the context of the community event. "It is through the subjugation of the individual will, in the service of community, that the greatest self-discovery is found." ◆

Leah Rugen is associate director of Expeditionary Learning Outward Bound.

Urban Exploration:
Making a Difference

Connie Russell-Rodriguez and April Cotte

Last spring the eighth grade at the Rafael Hernandez School in Boston embarked on an expedition that ultimately took on a life of its own. "Making a Difference: Urban Redevelopment through Activism" began as an attempt to design a new focus for our successful "Egleston Square Urban Rescue" project, so that it could be repeated for the sixth grade. We also wanted to incorporate a curriculum strand called "Immersion Journalism," which we learned through a seminar organized by PACE, an assessment project based at Harvard University in Cambridge. What began as separate pieces developed into an integrated experience of academic learning, character development, and risk taking.

We jumped into the spirit of activism by studying the Civil Rights movement, reading the biography of Harriet Tubman, and delving into the history of the women's movement and the struggle of the migrant workers. Rich information in these topics provoked lively and gripping discussions among the students and motivated them to want to find out more. We were careful to focus primarily on contributions of "ordinary people" in those historical events. We wanted to illustrate that it takes individuals who want to make a difference, and actually take a step, to create change in society.

We designed a two-day, overnight field experience—the Urban Exploration—where the familiar city environment would become new territory to explore in the context of activism and group living. That day we posed a challenge called an "Activist Quest." Students received the White Pages, a map, and only the *names* of activist organizations. Using these resources they had to decide which agencies to visit and in what order, how to get to them, and who would interview the people there. The agencies represent a variety of issues affecting people of diverse backgrounds and neighborhoods. To make the experience more workable and to encourage more group development, we divided the class in half, with ten people per group. Each group did a different Activist Quest.

We arranged parallel activities at different times for each group, providing them with similar stories

Rafael Hernandez School teacher Elaine Stanton and her students set out to monitor traffic on several Boston streets nearby the school during an expedition on transportation. Photograph by David Cornwell.

to share and comparisons to make. Each group helped prepare and serve food in a soup kitchen for about four hours. Each visited Chinatown, with the challenge of finding a sit-down meal of real Chinese food that would leave everyone satisfied for three dollars per person. We both visited the African Meeting House. Both groups had to plan an evening activity that related to the theme of activism. Finally, both groups had an "urban campout"; one slept in a church that functions as a school, and the other in a community agency's building—on the floor, of course!

We left on a Thursday morning and met back at school on Friday at about 4:00 P.M. The level of excitement in the class when we returned was indescribable. Perhaps a story that one group shared best illustrates the success of this trip.

Students explained that during their Activist Quest, as they walked along the sidewalk searching for the next agency, Maria came upon a bundle of bills and checks. "It's my money," she taunted, as she waved it in the air.

"I found it first," replied Angela, "but you pushed me out of the way to get it."

The rest of the group began to take sides. Some homeless people sitting on the curb held their tin cans up higher, and with their eyes open wide, followed the bills.

"You could give it to the hungry," suggested Raffi, still moved by the experience in the soup kitchen the night before. "No way!" shouted the other students, unconvinced.

"There is another option," interjected one of the instructors. "There is an address on the checks."

The group resisted this idea.

"He lost it. It's his bad luck."

"No one gives me back things when I lose them."

"That's not the way things are, not in my neighborhood."

"That's not the way things are . . . but could they be that way?" challenged the other instructor. It was an opportunity to make a difference. We could not have planned a greater learning opportunity.

During the ensuing conversation, a student offered the following definition of activism: "When you're in a situation and normally you would react in the same way as everyone else even though you know it's wrong, instead you do or say something different, something that will change it."

I wondered how different returning the money was for some of them. On almost every corner of this trip students came across learning opportunities,

ranging from whether or not to return lost money, to sneak onto the subway, to diss other ethnic groups, to work in a soup kitchen, to refer an addict to a detox. They even grappled over the way they treated each other.

The theme of the expedition was so powerful that when faced with unexpected situations, they automatically informed their decision-making process with their thoughts on activism. At some level, they

> The theme of the expedition was so powerful that when faced with unexpected situations, they automatically informed their decision-making process with their thoughts on activism.

◆ ◆ ◆

had taken a concept they had explored in the classroom and applied it to their own world. Activism was more than something historical figures participated in, more than even what they saw "other people" doing in the community; suddenly for students it was another way of looking at their own decisions.

The following Monday at school, we debriefed. When we asked the students for their ideas about the purpose of such an activity, we were surprised and thrilled to hear our goals as teachers being expressed by our students.

"So we could see how to change the community."

"To teach us to make decisions in a group."

"To see other parts of Boston that we didn't know about."

"To help the homeless."

"We became like junior activists," said one boy.

Inspired by the success of our first major activity, we went on to our next one. Diving into the waters of "Immersion Journalism," we arranged for each student to visit a member of the community whose work somehow serves the community. The students spent two working days with these people, shadowing them, observing their environment and their interactions, and interviewing them.

As we noted the trepidation with which they were approaching these visits, we realized that without conscious intention we had arranged the activities to mirror the Outward Bound sequence of the "training," "solo," and "final" expeditions. The first trip could be likened to the training expedition, where

◆ ◆ ◆

At some level, they had taken a concept they had explored in the classroom and applied it to their own world.

◆ ◆ ◆

students had the security of their fellow group members while they were charting the unknown territory of Boston activism. Now they were facing their "solo"—a trip they would take entirely on their own, outside the safety of the group, to find out how activism works in one person's life. Seeing their reactions at the end of the day only strengthened that metaphor; they were giddy and exhilarated, and simply would not stop talking, like people who have

taken a step outside their comfort zone and felt success. Even the next morning during math class, the teacher had to redirect them: "We'll have time to talk about your experiences this afternoon. Please pay attention!"

In the "final" phase of that sequence, students proposed and completed a community service project. They bubbled with ideas: "Can we go back to the soup kitchen?" "Could we go to work at a day care center?" Two boys designed and created a flyer for a basketball clinic for nine- to twelve-year-old children which they coordinated through the afterschool program of an agency they had visited. Not once did we hear "Do we have to?"

As we processed all the previous experiences of the learning expedition, we worked on our final project, a class-written, class-produced magazine entitled *Making a Difference*. Students wrote about historical figures they had studied, reviewed movies they had seen, wrote their reflections on the expedition, and reported on the agencies they had visited. In the context of the magazine these became letters to the editor, book and movie reviews, and editorials, among other things. Students wrote feature articles on the activists they had visited. Work went through numerous drafts, and students spent long hours at the computer. The students themselves learned to use the desktop publishing program and to design the pages.

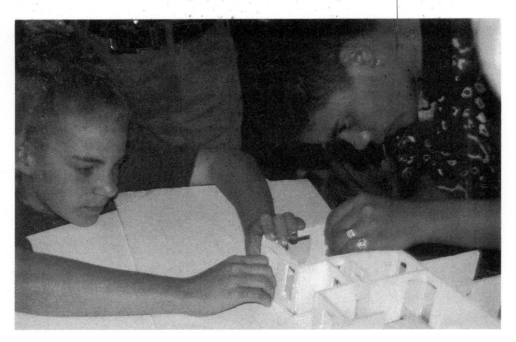

Laurie Tobias and Gilberto Baez of the Rafael Hernandez School in Boston construct an architectural model of a house for the service learning expedition "Egleston Square Rescue Project." Photograph by Annie Adamsky.

Despite the end-of-the-year madness common to us all, and that eighth-grade "attitude" that tends to pop up as graduation approaches, last summer we found the closing of the school year to be fun and productive.

◆ ◆ ◆

Gone was the typical cynicism of eighth graders who cannot wait to get out of middle school. It was replaced by the energized youth who have found that school really can have some meaning.

◆ ◆ ◆

Gone was the typical cynicism of eighth graders who cannot wait to get out of middle school. It was replaced by the energized youth who have found that school really can have some meaning. "Y'know what was cool?" said one student, after her community visit. "She was like a real person in the real world." This eighth-grade class made a connection between the history in books and the moments when they each take a step to make a difference. And we did not have to say a word. ◆

Author's note: As we look at making improvements for this year, it is notable that there are not significant changes to be made. We have added several weeks onto the expedition so as to provide adequate time for further revising and editing articles. We also found that the students needed more time and encouragement from us to complete their service projects successfully. Finally, based on suggestions from last year's students, we have decided to organize a luncheon for those community activists who so willingly give their time and energy, to recognize them and show our appreciation.

Connie Russell-Rodriguez teaches middle school at the Rafael Hernandez School in Boston, Massachusetts. April Cotte is an Outward Bound instructor at Thompson Island Outward Bound Education Center in Boston. Russell-Rodriguez led the expedition with her colleague Javier Mendez.

Students Designing for Students:

The Minisink Service Expedition

Joseph Newkirk

Our original idea was to be of service to the New York Mission Society. The Mission Society is the oldest private social service agency in New York City and is a partner of the School for the Physical City (SPC), serving as the parent, community, and family liaison. The Mission Society's Camp Minisink sits on two thousand acres a couple of hours north of New York City. During the first three days of June 1994, accompanied by parents and eight Cooper Union students, thirty sixth- and seventh-grade students from SPC participated in an overnight expedition to design cabins that would be considered for development on the campgrounds.

A project manager and an assistant project manager led groups of three to five students through the task of planning and generating the architectural design. A Cooper Union student joined each team to serve as a guide and to facilitate the learning process. In addition, the three-day expedition was an opportunity for parents to join in their children's learning process. Participating parents helped with logistics and guided students in constructing their cabin modules.

At Minisink, we started with a scavenger hunt designed to sharpen students' observational skills within the natural environment. Next, students had to articulate their aesthetic and emotional responses to their physical environment as they examined the camp and its cabins. A creative writing exercise, codesigned by then student-teacher Marianne Melendez, supported this process. The students reflected on the cabin designs by imagining how the main character from Ernest Hemingway's *Old Man and the Sea* would feel in them.

Students were engaged. One team devised a list of the advantages and drawbacks of building cabins on the existing wetlands, noting, for example, the risk of destroying animal life.

Scott Smith, a wildlife biologist from the New York State Department of Environmental Conservation, worked with the students around the theme of wetlands. First, he shared with them some of his concerns about building cabins on the wetlands.

The water provides a serene setting for two School for the Physical City students (New York) to share their reflections during the Minisink service expedition. Photograph by David Cornwell.

44

As teacher Laura Graves looks on, Jack Elementary School student James Creamer carefully saws a piece of wood as part of a service learning expedition. Photograph by David Cornwell.

Later, guiding students through the wetlands, Smith showed them how to test the sap from a yellow birch tree.

One architectural planning session engaged students in a discussion of the components of the cabins that they would design—layout, size, materials, utilities, function, and structure—and the function of the cabins in relation to space. Later, Al Isaac, an architect from the Salvadori Educational Center on the Built Environment, facilitated a discussion on planning. While learning about isometric plans, architectural plans, and elevations, the students brought their personal questions to the conversation. For instance, they thought about what rooms to include in the cabins. Then, equipped with architecture magazines, drafting boards, rules, and tape, the students began their group designs.

Critique sessions punctuated the expedition. First, students shared their individual design plans with their peers. They had to explain the conceptual thinking that led them to choose a particular design. Later critique sessions probed the analytic process of the groups. For example, one student team had drawn a circular building pattern. The students were asked whether or not this was an effective use of space. The project managers spurred their teams to rethink the designs collaboratively. One project manager lined up several designs on the drafting board and asked the team to consider which aspects of the designs could work together. In this way, the students completed their cabin designs.

Back at SPC, students had the opportunity to reflect on their experience at Minisink. The Expeditionary Learning design principles came alive in this expedition. For example, one student, reflecting on what it was like to work in the natural environment at Minisink, said, "It was peaceful and quiet and we got to do our work better." In addition, the experience required a lot of patience and cooperation. One student commented, "Working in groups was hard. We had to make a lot of decisions and there were a lot of arguments, but we had to complete something." The most important aspect of the experience, however, was the emphasis on self-discovery. Through hands-on learning, students could explore their capabilities. As one student concluded, "Anything is possible . . . we can do it even if we say we can't."

On June 20, students presented their cabin designs to members of the Mission Society's Board of Directors. We will return to Minisink next year to work on the second stage of the design. This will include redrafting cabin design, analyzing the site for development, and generating an environmental impact statement. This way students will continue their work from last year—students designing for students. ◆

Joseph Newkirk is an engineer and a middle school math and science teacher at the School for the Physical City in New York.

Can We Change the World?

Loretta Brady, with Denis Udall

In this narrative, humanities teacher Loretta Brady presents her learning expedition on social activism as a vehicle for change. She also describes strategies for helping students become better readers through discussing, reflecting on, and writing about a variety of texts, both fiction and nonfiction. Samples of writing from students in Brady's class are included in text boxes throughout the article.

A Thumbnail Sketch of the Expedition

The guiding questions of this expedition were, how do you know when it is time for change, and, what can people, including young people, do to bring about change? One of my goals was to move students from adolescent apathy to an understanding that while change is inevitable, it also depends significantly on who cares enough to control its direction.

At School for the Physical City in New York, teachers and students are constantly venturing into the city to learn and make meaning for themselves. This year we wanted to find ways of using the city as a venue for developing students' understandings of such disciplines as political change and conflict and compromise. The topic of change allows students wide opportunities to probe their curiosity, passions, and powers of inquiry. These are also the same characteristics students need to become independent thinkers and problem solvers.

I launched the class and got my students thinking about research topics by asking them if they believe they have the power to bring about change in the world. A number of students said, "I don't think we can do anything." Then I showed a videotape about a local youth empowerment group called Youth Force. It profiled six different local projects conceived and carried out by young people, such as taking back a park from crime and drugs, organizing rallies and concerts to benefit a cause, and exposing stores that sell alcohol to minors. When debriefing after the video the students said, "Well, of course they were brave. They had a lot of help. They could do those things because adults helped them. They didn't do it by themselves!" So I said, "Don't you think this school would get behind you?" And they responded, "Yeah, I guess. Sure."

Mark Weiss, principal of School for the Physical City, talks with students at a neighborhood playground in Manhattan. Photograph by Carrie Boretz for the New York Times.

Dear Mayor Giuliani,

I hope the voucher plan for NYC will help homeless out on the streets, because I would like to see a change in this confused city.

For our first expedition on activism and change, we recently visited The Coalition for the Homeless to find out why there are so many homeless still and how they can be cared for. We are also trying to find ways we can help.

It was all a great success. I, myself, gave food and clothes away. I was scared at first, but my friends encouraged me to go over to a lady who looked like she really needed my help. She had a big smile on her face when I came over, and that made me feel very happy. When I left, her friends started arguing, and I knew it was because of me and what I had given her. But what could I do?

Sincerely,
Miguel Maldonado

We also began to look at various artists who are trying to make change: for example, Michael Jackson's video *The Man in the Mirror*, and New York City mural artists. We visited the famous mural at the Pathfinder Bookstore and interviewed the volunteers there. When it was originally painted it was very controversial. Over the years it has been vandalized. The students got very interested and began to ask, "Who are all these people in that mural and why are they considered dangerous and controversial?" Meanwhile, in class we continued to examine art murals and their messages about the need for change. We also started working on our own mural. It contained slogans written by each student about something they wanted to change. For example, "They're building an incinerator in my neighborhood," and "I care about my family, but they're in trouble. They need support."

We also conducted several site visits. Experience has shown me it's best when the organizations we visit work on issues that are really hot. For example, there is a nursery that cares for AIDS babies—funded by both the government and the private sector—and they needed people to hug and play with their toddlers. In this way, the students can see firsthand what people are doing and realize that local activists and volunteers are working to make a difference. Young people often wonder where they fit into all this. The city's problems seem so overwhelming. They wonder if there is some way for them to get involved. Outward Bound reminds us that you have to help young people uncover their passion—not just a learning style, but a passion. If through their work they start to discover that inner fire, then they are better able to see the possibilities for making an impact in the world—not just painting park benches, but really important work.

Back in class, students selected an autobiography of someone who was involved in change, which they read on their own. We also began reading autobiographies of great leaders in order to look at what brought them to this work and what obstacles they overcame. The students were interested in examining not just politicians and activists, but also people who rose up to become leaders.

They wrote about their own experiences that were similar to those of the authors we were reading. I asked them, "Have you ever wondered about your own family the way Maxine Hong Kingston, author of 'No Name Woman' in *The Woman Warrior*, imagines what her aunt was like?" They had to select something that had happened to them earlier in their lives, and a more recent event, and then compare how they have changed. For example, José wrote about when, as a child, he learned to fear fire when he was burned over his entire back by a kettle of boiling water. And recently, as he sat by a campfire during an Outward Bound weekend trip, he relived those fears.

The Pathfinder Mural

. . . All of the faces I observed are people from all different nations who were trying to make peace by fighting for the rights of others. I thought about how much the world has changed since some of these activists worked. . . . I want to know more about everyone on this wall because many of them are very new to me, and I want to know why the book store worker said that people have tried to destroy this mural by throwing acid or eggs at it.

—Catherine McKeon

1939: War begins in Europe, by Ellison Fidler, a fourth-grade student at Clairemont Elementary School in Decatur, Georgia, drawn for a learning expedition on war and peace.

Dear Council Member Valone,

My class and I recently went to the Incarnation Children's Center, one of the many programs that will suffer greatly from the budget cuts. The babies were so much fun, and if some of them didn't have tubes sticking up their noses, you wouldn't have known they were sick. I was kind of depressed, but not as much as I thought I was going to be. I really want to go back there again because these kids were so nice, and they need someone our age to play with, so we were perfect.

I don't think making budget cuts from programs such as these will be a smart move. Many children will die from AIDS and other deadly viruses. If the cuts happen, 75 percent of the funds from the public will have to go. That would be bad news because people want to see more given to help others.

I know a person with AIDS who died before my ninth birthday. We had known he was going to die soon, and we were prepared for the worst, but that couldn't stop the outbreak of tears from my mom, and one or two from my dad, and only grief from me because I hadn't known him for very long.

Please reconsider how important nurseries like the Incarnation Center are and don't slash the budget.

Sincerely,
Sam Nathan

At the same time they were looking at their own lives. I asked, "What is something about yourself you've changed, or something you don't ever want to change?" These discussions and their reading led to our class book—a kind of memoir. Each student wrote a chapter about him- or herself. They wrote one chapter at the beginning of the year, another in January, and a third at the end of the year. Eventually, we published the memoirs. They are on loan, so people can borrow and read them. So in the end, the students were able to see change in their inner lives and their writing as a result of our work together, and how they used the lives of the people they studied to reflect on their own lives.

It's easy for me to get my students free-writing on a topic they care about. But where it gets hard for them is moving beyond the first draft into sculpting their pieces. To help them grasp the idea of revision I asked them, "What comes to mind when you hear the word *revision*?" They responded, "It's hard. It's tough. I hate it. Work." So I invited them to take a single piece of wire and shape it into a geometric shape or figure that said something about themselves, or expressed an emotion they were having. Then I asked them to change some aspect of it, give it a new shape. They went at it for hours. Some students asked for another piece of wire, but I insisted that they rework the one they started with. The sculptures went through many permutations. Then I asked them, "What does this shape mean or say to you?" and, "What are the similarities between this and revising?" One student wrote, "The world

Keith Studmire, Yasmin Peña, and Alisha Thompson of the Rafael Hernandez School in Boston pause to smile for the camera during a computer class. Photograph by David Cornwell.

> Our country is in a great dispute. And we have yet to see the promise of forty acres and a mule delivered to the ex-slaves who deserve to be compensated! Some Southerners say the land is theirs because they paid for it and ran the plantations. I understand all points, but what else can the former slaves do to live a good, honest life except raise crops? Didn't they work that land for no money? Besides, without giving them some land, most slaves will be homeless and poor. Life will be worse for everybody in the future. We should do what is best for the country.
>
> —Deena Schwartz

is mine soon, I hope." Another student produced a tangled piece of wire and wrote, "This is me, it's a knot. Because I'm in knots." His classmates asked him, "Why are you in knots?" And he said, "I don't know. I'm just tangled up inside all the time. I can't even see through it."

Later in the expedition, we looked at Reconstruction, following the Civil War, as a kind of failed activism. I started off by asking them to reflect about Reconstruction through the lens of several pieces of evidence: a photograph of a lynching, a story about two White, Northern teachers who moved to the South to teach former slaves and were run out of town, various quotations from the period, cartoons, and so forth. I invited them to pretend they were in the photo, or had taken it, and to write a story about what happened. This is often the most powerful entry point into a subject for my students; empathy and compassion are an important hook. An intellectual point of view is equally important—doubting and believing are strategies for trying to understand another point of view. But emotionally to place themselves in a scene or a historical moment can be a strong place to start from.

This led us to our culminating project based on their research: an activists' night. We put together an event for honoring, awarding, and recognizing people in the community who have done great things. We also presented our research on what still needs to be changed. Each humanities class at School for the Physical City was examining a different issue. One class looked at homelessness. Another focused on teen problems. They asked, "Are there enough jobs for teens? Are schools fair?

Are there enough good schools? Are there enough recreation programs?" There were a number of students who examined issues young women face growing up, especially single mothers. My own class was deeply interested in children and poverty, especially babies.

The activist night was a great success. There were posters and research papers up on the walls in a gallery format. People milled around while the students stood by their work and talked about it. There was also a slide show of the students' work on change and activism. The students presented short plays recreating scenes from the "activist" novelists they had read: *A Raisin in the Sun*, by Lorraine Hansberry, *Black Boy*, by Richard Wright, *Roll of Thunder, Hear My Cry*, by Mildred Taylor. They also presented monologues from autobiographies, like *The Good Times Are Killing Me*, by Linda Barry, *House on Mango Street*, by Sandra Cisneros, and *Mambo Month or Spicorama*, by John Leguizamo.

It's easy for me to get my students free-writing on a topic they care about. But where it gets hard for them is moving beyond the first draft into sculpting their pieces.

◆ ◆ ◆

The main presentation was a panel discussion made up of local activists. The students made speeches and presented awards to the activists. Herb Kohl gave the opening remarks on how you teach someone to be an activist and on why some periods are more full of activism than others.

Strategies for Teaching Reading

Within this complex, disciplinary expedition on political activism, I wanted to be sure my students were becoming stronger "activist" readers—able to reach in and grapple with, interrogate, exemplify, test, and refute the ideas of a writer. Increasingly, I am convinced that unless students can concretely track their own growth as readers, they will lack important information about how their own change as readers unfolds and builds. Through following the growth of their ideas and what they need to do when they get stuck, they can come to appreciate that a flexible, open mind is a more thoughtful and complex mind.

This has led me to an interest in how students read, how they think about what they read, and how they make sense of texts, especially nonnarrative

texts. They love rap sessions about hot general ideas, but they are not always reading closely and owning what they are reading. They are very comfortable winging things, but really using ideas—taking other people's ideas and using them to advance their thinking—is not familiar to them. This type of close reading requires that one enter

> I am convinced that unless students can concretely track their own growth as readers, they will lack important information about how their own change as readers unfolds and builds.

into a dialogue with oneself. I believe that thoughtful reading and writing are inseparable. I am interested in tracking this through the discussions they have with each other and in the writing they do after attending a seminar. What do the students gain by talking with others who have read the same thing they have? What is the effect on their writing?

Seminars, Press Conferences, Trials, and Debates

During a press conference, students propose ideas and try to persuade others to adopt their point of view, whether or not they actually believe in this particular position. The questions that the "press corps" asks should be aimed at trying to draw out the guest speaker to show his or her flaws or to challenge his or her thinking. They do not like that aspect of it because it is hard to take the perspective of someone you do not agree with. First you have to push yourself to agree with a viewpoint, and then you push to disagree with it. They are very good, natural thinkers. But they often need help thinking about and synthesizing knowledge—going beyond their experience and putting themselves in the place of an author, or putting themselves in the place of another person they may not agree with.

Dear Mr. Newkirk (SPC teacher),

Hi. I am studying for a term paper about the KKK and how to stop such violence against Black people today. What I found interesting is that the KKK claims to stand for Christianity, morality, and Americanism, yet all their methods prove they stand for exactly the opposite. Do you have any thoughts on how a person could believe that America is meant only for White Anglo-Saxon Protestants? Everything they stand for is against the Bill of Rights, what this country is based on.

I am wondering if anyone in your family had any experience with the KKK. When I first studied, I thought the KKK were only prejudiced against Blacks, but with more research I found that they are also anti-Catholic, anti-Semitic, anti-union. . . .

. . . I wonder what can be done to erase the fears of these people who are still active as KKK? How can we teach that the strength of America lies in her great ethnic diversity? I know that the Klan grew in strength when the fear of Communism was also at its height. Do we change them though education alone, or can we go as far as to outlaw their activities? They feel they have the right to infringe on the rights of people they consider un-American. I don't know how or what we can teach them, but we must never stop trying to conquer the fears of these people who hide under their masks. Our society has its problems, but they cannot be solved by segregation and bigotry. Mr. Newkirk, if you have any comments I would like to hear them.

Sincerely,
Evan Rodriguez

Joel Barsky reads with his students at the School for the Physical City in New York. Photograph by Carrie Boretz for the New York Times.

Helping students to argue from these various perspectives really deepens their writing. But I have found that they are not able to do it unless they have really taken the time to understand the background material they have read.

By contrast, in a Socratic seminar, the objective is to develop a shared understanding. We explore the topics until we resolve them. Students are critiqued for accuracy and analysis of the reading material. They are best at analysis. They really push each other. But they're not as good at collecting relevant evidence to support their ideas—taking a stance and being forced to develop it on their feet. Debates can encourage cheating. Sometimes the students go to any length to win, even if it means ignoring the evidence. Seminars, on the other hand, are more participatory. There is a mutual uncovering of a text.

It is interesting to see that students have begun to note that these different classroom approaches force different qualities of thought, or what the Coalition of Essential Schools calls *habits of mind*, one of which is evidence—demanding credible evidence to prove a position. We have conversations around questions like "Do you have enough evidence to back up your point of view?" and "How many examples do you need to support a supposition?" Where it gets hard for them is choosing the best evidence from what they have read or what they are learning.

At one point during a trial, things came to a head. The class stopped midstream. The students asked each other, "But wait a minute, what's a trial, anyway? What's a debate? What's a seminar?" When do we get to push our ideas? When do we want to find out the truth and use it to build an argument later?" They had to think about the different aspects of each. There are important differences among seminars, trials, and press conferences, such as the kinds of understandings they engender in students and the way they help students put their ideas together.

One thing these various teaching methods help with is students' tendency to cling to their own experience. It is hard for them to get outside of it. They think something is right, but they are not sure why. Or they don't know where they got an idea from, but they feel it viscerally and hang on to it anyway. I find that happens more often in debates. Sometimes debating makes them even more entrenched in their own views. Sometimes I turn their disagreements into questions. If they get locked in a heated discussion I try to open it up to a larger inquiry.

That technique worked in one mock trial. The students were exploring the meaning of the clause describing the equal "inalienable" right to a "pursuit of happiness" from the U.S. Declaration of Independence. Students read the oral history of

Linda Wright, a mother on public assistance who sued the federal government. Wright contended that the welfare system forced her to get off welfare and go to work as a jackhammer operator, rather than allowing her to go back to school to pursue her dream—to be a teacher. Thus, the government denied her the pursuit of happiness. After an embattled cross-examination, the room hotly divided by gender, I stopped the action to redirect the arguments into a more open-ended inquiry: "According to her own written testimony, when did the welfare hurt her, and when did it help her?" This shift made room for a more thoughtful analysis, not to mention a more compassionate tone.

We have a fairly standard format for trials. First, students choose sides and then begin looking over some articles I've brought in to prepare them. They list their questions and try to anticipate what the other side will say. Then they prepare their cross-examination questions. We also study other similar cases. They always ask me, "We should really know how other cases like this have been decided." So, for instance, for the trial of the welfare recipient they had to begin by asking themselves, "What is welfare? What is it supposed to do?" I find I need to do a lot of writing with my students before they make their arguments. The more I can get them to write beforehand, the stronger their opening statements are.

Second, they develop questions that will elicit what they want their witnesses to say on the stand.

> It is not as easy as people think it is to get recipients off public assistance. Out of my knowledge on welfare relief, I see that the problem is not so much getting recipients off the books, as it is a problem of creating good jobs, and helping people keep them. Based on three articles I read, out of the 65 percent who leave welfare relief programs, 45 percent return due to not being able to hold their jobs for reasons such as not making enough money for day care or rent. . . . The solution is to help support people in keeping a job and to make it profitable enough to make them want to work.
>
> —*Vijay Paltoo*

Their opening statements must tell their side of the story and help people anticipate what they will hear. And then in between are the cross-examinations and various expert witnesses. Finally, students have to write closing statements that attack the opposing view. This gives them a chance to reshape their arguments. Each time we do a trial, different students are defense and counsel. So by the end of the semester everyone has done one or the other at least once or twice. During the trial everyone who is not defense or counsel is a member of the jury. He or she is responsible for writing the opinion.

Rafael Hernandez School teacher Elaine Stanton explains to her students how to monitor traffic nearby the Boston school during an expedition on transportation. Photograph by David Cornwell.

Socratic Seminars Up Close

A Socratic seminar is based on student-centered critical reading in which the teacher never gives answers but facilitates through inquiry. During a seminar, each class member is equally responsible for the conversation. We tell the students there are a few ground rules: You cannot be part of the seminar if you do not come prepared. You cannot talk without having a firm grasp of the text. It is your responsibility to try to clarify your thinking. Do not stay confused. It is your job to ask questions and get help. The goal is to understand a value or idea in

In seminar, I train them to ask each other follow-up questions that clarify their main point: "Can you show me an example of what you're talking about? What evidence do you have for your statement?"

depth, not to get the right answer. Overall, these *habits of mind* do not usually come naturally to the students. They do not have a lot of patience for really understanding an idea in all its complexity. It is hard for students really to work at something before they talk. They would rather shoot from the hip and have a rap discussion.

Sometimes our seminars are organized around aphorisms. For example, "the survival of the fittest." We asked ourselves, "Should this law hold true for humans, as well as the natural world?" This forced us to define what we meant by "survival" and "the fittest." It helps to begin with these more contained discussions because our students are still not sure how to use examples and counter-examples or how to go about analyzing a question and defining terms. So a good part of the process is just learning how to formulate a rich question. Finding the answer is another thing. It's an exercise of taking these various views, finding out where your argument has gaps, and being able to characterize that in a way that leads somewhere.

For students, there is an interesting interplay between expressing their opinions and ideas and then having to find outside sources to help sort out what they believe. That is really what seminar is all about. They have read the U.S. Constitution before, but unless they really work with those ideas they will not own them.

A lot of the job is working with them to clarify their questions. In seminar, I train them to ask each other follow-up questions that clarify their main point: "Can you show me an example of what you're talking about? What evidence do you have for your statement? Who disagrees?" Questions like these help them flesh out their ideas and begin to see the places where they agree. So it's not just me saying, "No, you're wrong. Because I know." I say, "Let's find out. Are you really sure? How do you know that? Why don't we research this to see if it has some truth?" These inquiries reinforce my use of the *habits of mind*, which include making connections, exploring one's assumptions and different points of view, and seeking relevance, alternatives, and evidence.

All of this discussion leads to a place where students are less positional and dogmatic than you might expect from this age group. They are a little bit more willing to listen to others and give examples in a way that sheds a different light on the subject. In other words, there is less competitive rigidity, and less talking past one another.

We usually prepare a lot before a seminar. Again, the more they have thought and talked about the issues, the richer the discussions. For instance, before one seminar we read a set of writings from social commentators, Michael Harrington and Alex Kotlowitz. Each author had a different perspective on the question of whether people are inherently selfish. The students underlined parts they found interesting and kept track of their questions. Their questions were great: "If the poor were so invisible, then how did Harrington, a middle-class White man, learn about them?" "If these poor folk are so stuck and no one is helping them, why don't they just pick up and move somewhere else?" In between the readings they interviewed their family members on these questions: "Do you think people are more selfish now or at some earlier time? Do you think kids are more selfish than adults? In general, do you think people are selfish?" Then I asked them to write an essay about which of the three arguments they found most compelling. So by the time they came to the seminar they had really done a lot of thinking and were ready to express their point of view.

Socratic Seminar: What Is Liberty?

This discussion followed a close reading of an excerpt of John Locke in which he describes the need for a government as a contract, by consent, deriving its authority from the agreement of the people.

Arlander: Listen, listen, so he's saying . . . What if you have a mugger who holds you up with a gun and takes your wallet and all your money. He has power but not authority.

Ali: No, no, no. He has power *and* authority. He can have both.

Arlander: No, but you have to agree that . . . yes, "you can have my wallet 'cause your family is poorer than mine. . . ."

Ali: No, no.

Vijay: So you're saying . . . it's like, Loretta has authority but not power because we agree to let her rule . . . she's helping us learn . . .

Ali: No, no. They both have power and authority. They can make you do something you don't want you do. The mugger has a gun . . .

Arlander: Okay, now listen, what if the mugger gets caught by the police. Police have power and authority [according to Locke].

Lydia: Yeah, well sometimes the police have only power and not authority. Power corrupts. Just look at the government we have.

Arlander: Okay, what if the policeman grabs the mugger, punches him when he's on the ground and beats his head in. Just because the government—I mean we—agreed to let the police protect us, can he do that?

Loretta: What would Locke say?

Vijay: Hold on, wait a minute. All of these "what ifs"—what if this, what if that. He can't do that, can he, Loretta? We'll go on forever! Enough already, Arlander!

Loretta: Actually, isn't that one of the ways people come to understand what they think and believe? Arlander is doing something very important in the seminar. After all, how else could our revolutionary U.S. founding documents have lasted if the original authors didn't test their ideas as you are?

I can really see the difference in a piece of writing when we haven't talked about the subject students are writing about either in a seminar or some other setting. On the other hand, when we have thoroughly discussed a text before coming to seminar, they often need help afterward returning to the text to look for evidence to support their claims. Otherwise they are likely to go no further than where they ended up at the close of the seminar. So there has to be an interplay between the two.

I am realizing that while they are good at using quotations from the text to back up their arguments, they are much better at this when writing about a historical event than they are when advancing their own ideas. Also, those students who are beginning to learn to use quotations struggle with how to pick the best ones. They often select the most emotional—the raw feeling of the freedom rider under attack by white racists—rather than a quotation that has analytical power.

Sometimes I am surprised I have to wean them away from research that is limited to fact finding.

There needs to be a marriage between an impressionistic approach and a research paper that has facts with little of their own voices in it.

Overall, I am surprised how they use the seminar to connect what they have done during the week. I wonder if the fact that I have placed the seminar at the end of the week has anything to do with it. They can draw upon what we've studied earlier in the week, so the conversations are more informed and focused. It's interesting that they can start pulling in what they have been working on. It also helps me to move from more concrete ideas to abstract ones over the course of the week. So we have the more concrete press conference, or reading group discussions in the beginning of the week, and then the seminar at the end incorporates what the students have been working on during the week and can be raised to a higher level. ◆

Loretta Brady is a humanities teacher at School for the Physical City in New York. Denis Udall is a school designer with Expeditionary Learning Outward Bound.

Part Three

Weaving in Standards and Assessment

The children not only seem to be motivated, they also are making decisions and choices. At a very early age, the students learn the process that takes place from rough draft to a more polished form, and they take pride and satisfaction from this.

—Teacher
Academy for Educational Development Evaluation

Through Lines:
Evolving Standards and Assessment

Mieko Kamii

It has been a year since we began the conversation about standards and assessment in these pages, and in that year much has transpired, both in our schools and across the nation. This year, since much of our energy will be focused on developing the classroom and school cultures that support student achievement of high standards, we thought an update and synthesis on standards and assessment was timely. Because standards and assessments are an integral part of the overall philosophy and methods of Expeditionary Learning's design, not something added on or standing apart, we start with some assumptions.

We assume that the key to transforming America's schools is infusing our schools with the new energy and excitement that comes from constant challenge and achievement. Nothing of importance will happen in our schools until classrooms become places where teachers and students alike want to be. Teachers and students are actively *co-constructing* knowledge, carrying out investigations at the edge of certainty and understanding. The results matter; the work is demanding yet rewarding and fun.

The energetic atmosphere of challenge and excitement we have in mind will not come about through mere "reform." We are aiming at a revolution in the culture of education in our schools: away from the passive mode of learning where teachers are encouraged to accept prepackaged curricula delivered to their desks by "experts" and in turn deliver them to the desks of their students; away from the convention of changing teachers every year where teachers are robbed of the opportunity to witness students' growth over time and where relationships with students and their parents begin anew each fall; away from the isolation that too often prevails, each

Illustration of zebra by Cynthia Ocasio, a third grader at the Rafael Hernandez School in Boston, for a learning expedition on mammals.

Zebra foal

teacher in her or his classroom, where community is little more than hurried words in the hallway en route to the office; away from educational decisions by distant authorities who rarely traverse the classrooms and playing fields of the school.

We are persuaded that the level of performance of teachers and students can be raised only by creating a context in which both are drawn creatively into the design of their own educational programs.

Second, we assume that education will remain decentralized in the United States, with each state and community imposing its own judgments about what the major obstacles are that its students must face and what standards they ought to achieve. Consequently, the core of our design must be flexible, adaptable, and open to revision, and this applies to our schemes for standards and assessments as well.

Not least, we are persuaded that education cannot be enjoyable for teachers or students so long as assessment looms as a climactic and dreaded event,

inhibiting the initiative of teachers, intimidating students, and producing little in the way of feedback for improving the quality of either one's work.

The basic tools intended to achieve the goal of revolutionizing the culture of education in our schools are learning expeditions and portfolios, and they are central to our approach to standards and assessment as well.

Learning expeditions—thematic, interdisciplinary, project-based courses of study—form the curricular core in our schools. Learning expeditions are planned and implemented by teachers who have thought about how their teaching contributes to the community's expectations of what students should know, be able, and be disposed to do. Embedded in every learning expedition are extended projects that require students to develop, over time, the literacy, communication, research, analytical, artistic, technical, interpersonal, and other skills the community values. Students' works—the demonstration of these skills—are held in classroom "working folders" so that the pieces can be revisited and revised until students and teachers feel they are "done."

◆ ◆ ◆

Building an understanding of oneself as a learner enables one to experience greater autonomy and to assume more responsibility for learning.

◆ ◆ ◆

King Middle School student Kim Dame builds a wooden model of a carnival ride in Will Pidden's technology class in Portland, Maine.

Portfolios are instruments for demonstrating the quality of students' work. Portfolios consist of selections from students' working folders which they themselves have chosen for particular purposes or as demonstrations of specific skills. The student includes an explanation of why he or she has selected specific works and what the works, singly or in combination, are intended to show. This corpus forms the evidentiary base for determining how far individual students have progressed toward meeting community standards. Thus portfolios function in our design as tools of standards and assessment.

Baltic Isopod sketch by Perry O'Brien, a seventh-grade student at King Middle School, for the marine biology learning expedition of Casco Bay.

Portfolios are more than collections of student work to be used for evaluative purposes. Not only do they contain the evidence of individual students' accomplishments for others to see, they also give students real data to reflect upon as they come to understand themselves as thinkers, knowers, producers, learners: "Why did I select this particular piece of work to include in my portfolio?" "What does it show?" "How well does it meet the standards?" "What was easy or difficult, enjoyable or onerous for me?" "Where did I put in my greatest effort?" "Why am I proud of it?" "If I had the chance, how would I extend this work?" The ability to assess our own work against standards means we have engaged with the standards, that we have come to understand what they mean and what the community values. In a similar vein, building an understanding of oneself as a learner enables one to experience greater autonomy and to assume more responsibility for learning.

Portfolios also provide data for teachers' reflections upon their own work. Teachers can ask of themselves, or better yet of one another as they collectively review the student portfolios from a colleague's class, "What patterns do I see in students' learning, understanding, achievement?" "What are the successes and where are there holes?" "Is there evidence that some students are being better served than others? That some topics are being better taught than others?" "What can be done to remedy the apparent shortcomings?" Conversations such as these, carried out among colleagues, in which teachers engage in mutual inquiry and assist one another by sharing insights about teaching and learning, are part of our broader scheme for enriching the sense of community within a school.

These are but some of the ways that portfolios, hand-in-glove with learning expeditions, function as provocation for revolution in the culture of the schools that we intend. We turn now to a more specific discussion of the development of standards and frameworks for assessment.

Standards

Initially our design called for standards in the following seven areas which were drafted to respect the interdisciplinary, project-based focus of learning expeditions. Benchmarks were to be established at grades three, eight, and twelve. As nationally developed content standards and state curriculum frameworks are published, and as discussions of performance standards in all of the Expeditionary Learning schools progress, the standards embraced by individual Expeditionary Learning schools will naturally undergo reformulation, refinement, and revision so that at each site, the standards truly reflect the needs and expectations of the state and local communities of which they are a part.

Communication. Communication involves making meaning for oneself as well as conveying meaning to others. Communication is used for a variety of purposes and takes place in a variety of modes. In today's world, effective communication includes fluency in a second or even third language.

Character and work habits. Character and work habits refer to habits of mind, of heart, and of hand, nurtured and developed over time, which emerge for analysis and reflection in students' ongoing work and everyday lives. Habits of mind, heart, and hand include *values* such as honesty, fairness, equity, tolerance, and respect for persons, property, and the natural world; *dispositions* such as courage, resoluteness, compassion, thoughtfulness, perseverance, doing one's best, and expecting high-quality products and performances from oneself; and *capacities* such as effective teamwork, communication, and organization of time and tasks.

Quantitative reasoning. Quantitative reasoning engages problem-solving strategies, and includes creating relationships among quantifiable phenomena and communicating mathematical ideas using multiple representations. It involves making connections between mathematical ideas and those encountered in the sciences, social sciences, humanities, and arts, and using them to study real-world problems.

Scientific thinking and technology. Scientific thinking undergirds scientific inquiry, experimentation as a mode of studying "answerable" questions, respect for evidence, thinking analytically and critically about data, and suspending judgment until alternative possibilities have been explored. It involves consideration of how science both transforms and is transformed by the world we live in. Technology creates possibilities for making new knowledge, communicating information, and producing things.

Cultural, geographic, and historical understanding. Cultural, geographic, and historical understanding highlights the necessity of viewing people, places, objects, events, and beliefs from multiple perspectives, whether in historical or contemporary times. It underscores the constructed and contextual nature of knowledge, and encourages the interrogation of all cultural myths, beliefs, and creations.

Arts, aesthetics, and literature. Arts, aesthetics, and literature call attention to recognizing and transforming human experiences into artistic forms of expression, and gaining from these expressions greater insights into the meaning of human existence. Included here are music, the visual arts, dance, theater, poetry, and other artistic modes of communication.

Fitness. Fitness refers to physical and socioemotional health and well-being, or knowing about, respecting, and protecting one's body, spirit, and social relationships. Included here are physical dimensions such as exercise, nutrition, and protection against disease and pregnancy, and socioemotional aspects such as maintaining healthy habits of mind, social relationships, and relationships with nature.

Classroom Assessment

We have proposed the adoption of a four-part framework for assessment in the classroom consisting of

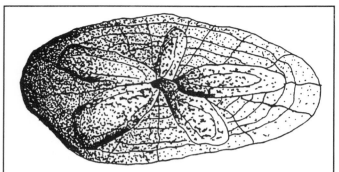

Common Sand Dollar (Echinarachnius parma).

General Physical Description: The Sand Dollar has a thin, flat, and circular body. It is about two to four inches wide and looks like a silver dollar or cookie. The top surface of the sand dollar has a set of breathing tubes that are arranged in the form of a five-point star. Its body is covered with tiny spines, which are used for crawling and digging. It also resembles a flattened sea urchin.

Habitat: Sand Dollars live on firm sand in sheltered waters, northward from Long Island, New York. They are found on the beach all along the coast of the Atlantic Ocean.

Food Eaten: The Sand Dollar's food consists of tiny bits of plants found among the sand grains. The food travels along the grooves on the underside of the sand dollar's body to its mouth. They also feed on organic material and plankton. Cilia on the small spines of the sand dollar move these food particles until they are trapped by mucus around the spines and are pushed into the mouth of the organism.

Role in the Food Chain: Sand Dollars are eaten by fish that eat off the bottom of the ocean such as cod, flounder, and haddock. Other predators are starfish and sea urchins. Sand Dollars are near the bottom of the food chain.

Reproductive Life: The Sand Dollar sheds either eggs or sperm into the surrounding water. They do this from their five gonads, which open through five holes in the upper disc. Fertilization takes place in the water. The larva develops and drifts in the current for many weeks before they grow and settle on the sea floor.

Human Interactions: After a day at the beach, the most rewarding thing to find is a Sand Dollar in the sand. Many people collect them as a hobby. Also, an indelible ink is prepared from Sand Dollars. It is made by pounding a sand dollar into powder in water.

Geographic Range: They are found from the sandy shore of Maine to Mexico and California.

Status: Sand Dollars are abundant on sandy bottoms of oceans.

Life Span: The Sand Dollar's life span depends on the temperature of the water they live in. They grow faster in warmer climates but they have a shorter life span than in colder climates. However, in colder climates they have a longer life span but they grow more slowly. Some Sand Dollars are known to live for more than eight years.

Common Sand Dollar, by Maggie Connolly, a seventh grader at King Middle School in Portland, Maine, for "The Ocean: What's Under There?" a field guide to the Gulf of Maine.

incidental, ongoing, culminating, and external forms of assessment.

For the most part, incidental assessment refers to the recording of observational data by the teacher as he or she circulates among the students and sees who among the group understands or is having difficulty with a lesson or task. Incidental assessment may include on-the-spot running records of students' behavior, questions, or problem-solving strategies during small group work, and checklists of specific acquisitions (for example, particular reading or writing skills) they have demonstrated. In contrast to the next three types, this form of assessment is teacher initiated and controlled.

Ongoing forms of assessment engage students in thinking analytically about their own and others' work, in experimenting with alternative solutions to problems (for instance, another solution procedure for a math problem, another idea for an ending to a short story, another way of recording the results of a science experiment, another approach to a design problem), and in revising their work. Examples of formats for ongoing assessment include student-teacher and peer conferences, small- and large-group critique sessions, and opportunities for reflection on the feedback students have received.

Several points bear mentioning in conjunction with ongoing forms of assessment. First, it is by discussing specific aspects of a student's work that performance standards become clarified, not only for the student whose work is under review, but also

Students' revisions will be as good as the quality and specificity of the feedback given to them, coupled with their ability to understand the suggestions they receive.

for the group as a whole. Second, ongoing assessment is indistinguishable from sensitive instruction. Students must be actively engaged in the conversation and really be listening (and listened to) if they are to benefit from the questions, suggestions, or objections they receive. Third, students' revisions will be as good as the quality and specificity of the feedback given to them, coupled with their ability to understand the suggestions they receive. Students need to feel encouraged and supported to launch on yet another draft. Fourth, students need to be exposed to many models or exemplars of high-quality work and to be able to discuss and debate what it is about those works that make them so good (standards). Finally, when a classroom "culture of revision" is established, students will have become accustomed to the notion that in their class, students exert themselves, work hard, and are satisfied only when they have done their best work.

Culminating assessments centering on students' portfolios may serve any one of a number of purposes. Students might assemble portfolios to introduce themselves to a next teacher and therefore include in them an autobiography, works that show special interests and preferences, and reflections on

Cooper Union design school graduate student Athena Carmicheal works with School for the Physical City (New York) teacher Joseph Newkirk during the Minisink service expedition. Photograph by David Cornwell.

Artwork by Cody Hitchcock, a third grader at Clairemont Elementary School in Decatur, Georgia, for the class book for the "Habitat" learning expedition.

both their weaknesses ("where I need help") and strengths as learners. A second type is an end-of-the-year "showcase portfolio" that consists entirely of a student's "best works." A third type of selection process involves making additions to and deletions from a cumulative portfolio that is intended to be a record of a student's progress and growth over several years. Another type, and one that goes beyond the individual classroom, is a portfolio that is assembled for the purposes of broad-based external school review (for example, Kentucky Mathematics Portfolio) or for the purposes of obtaining individual student scores (for example, New Standards Portfolio Assessment in English Language Arts). Here, students are asked to submit specified pieces of work that reflect their efforts to meet particular standards *after* they have worked with the rubrics that are to be used in scoring the work (see the discussion of "cross-site assessment," below). Thus the review, selection, and reflection processes will vary, depending upon the purpose and audience for the portfolio review.

Finally, portfolio presentations and exhibitions of final projects may be the focus of external assessment. Parents, community members, or teachers and students from other schools are invited to participate in a review process that enables students to present their work and receive valuable feedback from people beyond the school.

Portfolio Cultures

Of utmost importance at this juncture is understanding what it takes to establish portfolio cultures within our schools and why this is important. Portfolio cultures are ones in which the boundaries between instruction and assessment are indistinct. In the words of Dennie Wolf, "Assessment becomes an episode of learning." The goals of assessment in such a culture are scaffolding students' learning, facilitating their development of important concepts and skills, providing students with the best tools and supports we can imagine for improving the quality of their work, and deepening students' thoughtfulness as they (and we) walk up to hard questions and nettlesome problems. These goals are one and the same with the instructional goals of many if not most teachers.

Portfolio cultures are ones in which the boundaries between instruction and assessment are indistinct.

◆ ◆ ◆

To embrace the notion that virtually all children can learn and achieve high standards is to admit past shortcomings in our understanding of how to teach, scaffold, and facilitate the learning of vast numbers of students. Portfolio cultures provide one means of challenging ourselves to do better, to make explicit the criteria by which we judge successful performances, and to find ways of helping less successful or less confident students close the gap between what they are currently doing and what they should aim to accomplish. Establishing a classroom culture of revision in which the goal is for everyone to achieve high performance standards, regardless of how much time and effort it takes, is one step. Figuring out what kinds of feedback are most helpful for different kinds of learners, or for the same learner at different points in time, is another. Again, this lies at the heart of instructional endeavors.

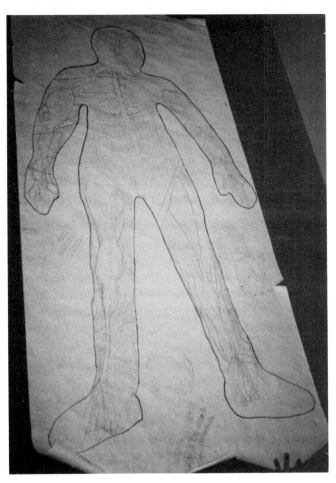

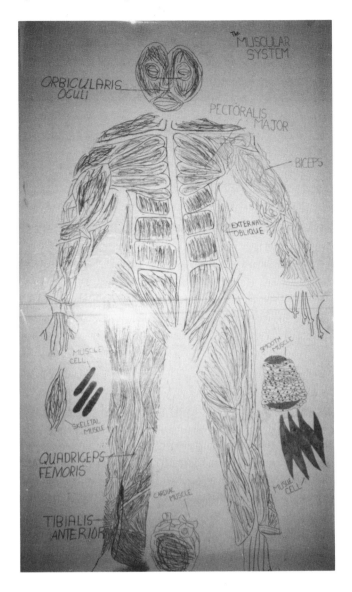

The photograph on the left represents the Clairemont Elementary School (Decatur, Georgia) students' work in its early stages before the class held a critique session with a health professional. The photograph on the right illustrates the significant improvement after the students revised the work based on the feedback. Photograph by Vivian Stevens.

Perhaps the biggest shift for schools to make is to understand the difference between traditional purposes of assessment—ranking and sorting—and assessment that supports teaching and learning, and to find the courage and the means to do whatever they can to embrace the latter. Learning expeditions and portfolio cultures were made for one another. We are challenged to find a way of permanently marrying the two.

Cross-Site Assessment

How do we know that a portfolio score of 4 or 5 on a five-point scale means the same thing in Portland as it means in Denver or Dubuque? How are the scales established? And how are the standards, fleshed out in the rubrics, determined in the first place?

In order to judge the quality of a performance or a portfolio against specified standards, and to let students know what they have to do in order to improve their work, teachers and researchers have developed rubrics or specifications of the qualities that distinguish one level of performance from another, most widely in writing and reading but more recently in other areas such as mathematics and science. Once a group of teachers has been immersed in using a reasonably well-developed rubric, the teachers have been able to score reliably portfolios (and performance tasks) of students they have never taught, never met. The purpose of using rubrics is to assess the quality of work done by students who have not necessarily done the same assignments, read the same books, or had the same field experiences. Rubrics allow these students' portfolios to be evaluated along common dimensions.

The process of writing standards and developing rubrics is laborious but necessary if our goal is to assess complex and varied performances rather than the sorts of knowledge and skills picked up extremely cheaply and adequately, using multiple choice, bubble sheet formats.

The process of developing these instruments is roughly as follows. Local schools, districts, or states figure out who should be involved in setting standards (teachers, parents, members of local governing boards, central office and community representatives, specialists in the disciplines from colleges or universities, and so forth). The group is convened and decides how its work will proceed (formation of subcommittees, setting of timetables, writing of agendas, agreement on discussion formats, and the like). The group or subgroup studies examples and models of standards and rubrics that have been developed elsewhere. The groups then develop their first drafts of standards in the agreed-upon areas (as a starting point, the seven areas specified earlier in this document) and assemble samples of student work that are used to assess whether the standards make sense. The next phase consists of looking at student work and drafting the rubrics that specify the criteria that will be used in assessing future work (again, rubrics outline levels of performance in achieving the kinds or qualities that "count" in meeting a standard). Next, a collection of student work is scored to see how well the rubric works in the light of real student performances. This leads to the first round of revision of the rubric, which is subsequently tried with yet another collection of student work. The process continues until the scorers are satisfied with a "final" version of the rubric.

As these discussions proceed, teachers and other community members who are involved in the process of setting standards and writing rubrics inevitably become engaged in conversation over their differences of opinion. In setting standards, the group discovers that the ideas of the business manager, the theater director, and the English language arts teacher differ with respect to valued aspects of "communication." These conversations are extremely important. It is instructive and thought-provoking for persons inside and outside of schools or academic departments to hear what others think. Likewise, a group of middle-school science teachers who are charged with writing a rubric for scoring science portfolios may discover that what one teacher emphasizes in assessing student work is markedly different from another. Such discoveries can lead to rich conversations not only about teaching but also about the disciplines themselves.

School Review

How do we engage the public not only in understanding the kind and quality of education taking place in our schools, but in soliciting feedback on which aspects of students' schooling are working well and which areas deserve greater clarity or attention? One structure for simultaneously providing public accountability and receiving specific and useful feedback is to ask a visiting panel to do an in-depth review of the school. The panel would be composed of interested citizens and stakeholders and would include teachers, administrators, and parents from other schools; personnel from the central office; a member of the school board, city council, or state department of education; and others concerned with the quality of teaching and learning going on in the school.

◆ ◆ ◆

Thoughtfully done, standards and assessments are powerful allies in revolutionizing the culture of education in our schools.

◆ ◆ ◆

To begin the visit, teachers, parents, and administrators would discuss with the panel what they see as the strengths of the school, areas in which progress is being made, and their strongest concerns. The panel would be asked to do classroom observations and then read and score a stratified random sample of portfolios. To do this, the portfolios of every student in the school would be assembled in a room and divided by the teachers into categories of strong, medium, and weak work, according to the teachers' assessment. The review panel members would be acquainted in advance with the appropriate rubrics, and would randomly select and score portfolios from each of the categories. Then they would confer with the students' teachers to discuss their findings—compliments, criticisms, and questions.

The final stage of such a review would involve a presentation of findings to the whole faculty, at the end of which everyone would be invited to raise questions, clarify misunderstandings, express uncertainties, and give thanks. The faculty would then use the results to select major issues to work on during the ensuing months or year. Arrangements would be made for the panel to return the following year or at the end of the second year to offer its assessment of what had changed in the school.

The review process sketched above borrows from the practices of university and school accrediting bodies in the United States, Her Majesty's Inspectorate in the United Kingdom, and the Southern Maine Partnership. There are several benefits to this process. A school receives an independent evaluation of how well it is matching expectations of the wider community; feedback is immediate and focused on the school's specific situation and practices; teachers, administrators, and parents publicly share their impressions and concerns and receive validation for their work; and the school personnel and the wider public are given an occasion to affirm their mutual understanding of the tasks the school must next address. In this process the school is given an opportunity to demonstrate its accountability while drawing the public into its core.

Supporting Activities

The Cambridge office of Expeditionary Learning Outward Bound will support the development of standards and assessments in the sites in several ways. It will help local participants understand the value of articulating standards and making the criteria for meeting them public. It will assist in explaining the connection between developing a portfolio culture and a classroom culture of revision and high standards. It will provide suggestions for discipline-specific as well as multidisciplinary standards.

The Cambridge office will support local and cross-site professional development activities aimed at developing and revising standards and scoring rubrics (drafting standards; looking at student work; drafting rubrics; scoring student work against the rubrics; revising the standards and/or rubrics), and will make every effort to provide access to teachers for professional development opportunities organized by others (for instance, the Four Seasons Project, NCREST). It will also assist schools in designing school review processes and procedures.

Since administrative and methodological problems with performance assessments still have to be resolved, it is premature to depend exclusively on them for high stakes and for accountability purposes. In the meantime there is little choice but to continue to administer whatever standardized multiple choice, bubble sheet tests (for example, Iowa Test of Basic Skills, California Achievement Tests, Metropolitan Achievement Tests, and the Regents Competency Tests) are sanctioned by local districts. It is important to understand that for the purposes of comparing schools, these tests should not be administered in their entirety to every student every year. The use of matrix random sampling will cut the time students spend actually completing the exams. Teachers will still be obligated to devote class time to "test-taking skills," a practice that will at least prepare students for taking the SAT and similar kinds of exams.

The realm of standards and assessments is alive these days with vigorous and consequential debates. Expeditionary Learning is attentive to these debates and remains open-minded about new insights that may emerge from them. We are persuaded that the design we have sketched out incorporates important virtues and remains flexible enough to adapt to new findings. We believe our design incorporates the most fundamental truth: that if thoughtfully done, standards and assessments are powerful allies in revolutionizing the culture of education in our schools. ◆

Mieko Kamii is director of standards and assessment for Expeditionary Learning Outward Bound.

Practitioners Discuss Portfolios:

Your Best Work Is What's Expected of You

Mieko Kamii

---

*As part of a recent conference on portfolio assessment, six panelists responded to a series of questions posed by conference participants for discussion. The panelists were **Ron Berger**, Shutesbury Elementary School (Shutesbury, Massachusetts); **Loretta Brady**, School for the Physical City (New York City); **Julie Craven**, research associate, PACE (Performance Assessment Collaboratives for Education), Harvard Graduate School of Education; **JoAnne Eresh**, writing coordinator, Pittsburgh Public Schools; **Kathy Greeley**, Graham and Parks School (Cambridge, Massachusetts); and **Linda Nathan**, codirector, Fenway Middle College High School (Boston). The panel was moderated by **Mieko Kamii**.*

What kind of teaching or classroom culture has to be present before portfolios can flourish?

Berger: There are no preconditions in classroom culture for bringing in portfolios. Wherever you are, bring portfolios in and get things going.

However, I don't think portfolios are a neutral structure. I think they call for a certain kind of classroom curriculum, and they don't work well with others. I have a very strong prejudice, and it is toward original student work. If students are learning and demonstrating their skills through original work, the portfolios will be rich and diverse. And if they're not, the portfolios are going to be pretty weak.

Even if your school culture or classroom culture is not based in original work, bringing in portfolios will start pushing it in that direction. Frankly, if you had a bunch of portfolios full of work sheets, or

responses to prearranged standardized texts, the portfolios wouldn't be very interesting to look at. I think portfolios are an engine pushing staff toward looking at "What's original in the work? How are portfolios pushing students to do something that's distinctive and that's their own?"

There are no preconditions in classroom culture for bringing in portfolios. Wherever you are, bring portfolios in and get things going.

—Ron Berger

Brady: This is a very time-intensive process, so we'd better be assessing what we really care about the most. At our school, we decided that analytic reading at the middle and high school levels is what we care about. Then we realized we were assessing something we weren't teaching as well as we wanted. And so we have been learning how to teach it better. It's so important to get clear about what standards look like along the way.

How do you set up a safe climate for peer review?

Greeley: Right now I have probably the toughest class I've ever had in terms of how they treat each other. How do we establish respect in the classroom? It really had to start from day one, saying, "We are here as a community of learners." We talked about how we are empowered to do amazing things when we can work together as a team and have safety with each other. We went back and looked at how we feel when we feel safe and respected, and what we are empowered to do. We looked at what happens to us when we are really shut down and feel unsafe, or when people don't want to listen to us.

I used to think there was some kind of magic required. I'd go into Ron's classroom, and I'd see students giving each other incredible feedback and support, and I'd go into other classrooms and see students working together and think, "Well, they did something magical."

68

Student Jason Bowen is immersed in his work at the drafting table during a Portland Arts and Technology High School expedition on architecture. Photograph by Scott Hartl.

It finally hit me with my class this year. It isn't magic. It is constant, ongoing, hard work. Anytime there's any kind of dispute or put-down, you stop. You talk about what the cost to the whole community was. "You just took something away from everybody. It means we can't move forward into these great spaces that we're headed for."

Before we talk about critique, we go over the rules: "Why do you do critique?" It makes work better. Writers do it for each other because they're looking to make their work better. They aren't looking to make the author feel better as a person. We're looking to make the work better. So we want first to support the writer and tell the writer what we appreciate in his or her work.

I tell them, "This is not just to make you feel better. It's because I want you to learn to articulate what's good. There's always something good to recognize, and the more we can identify the strength

in work, the more we can own that strength." That's always the first step, and I am absolutely rigid about it. A student will read a three-sentence essay, and the other students will say, "How are we going to find something good in that?" We'd better find something good in there.

The next step is moving to asking questions and not criticizing. We're in the middle of parent-teacher student conferences right now, and one of the parents said, "I'm so amazed at how open Jonathan is to people's input on his work."

Jonathan said, "Well, you know this is the first time where I didn't feel like people were jumping in and telling me everything that was wrong. First they always tell me something that's good, and that makes me feel really good. And then people don't tell me what to do; they give me suggestions."

But what I have really learned is that it's every day. It's constant; it's holding students to a really high standard of being kind and supportive to each other and understanding that when we are, it empowers us to do tremendous things together.

Craven: Critiquing is a skill. You're teaching people how to do it, and it doesn't happen on day one.

First, we need clarity about criteria and standards. You feel safe if you know that criticism will stay within certain bounds. In my class, students do an oratory. We look at examples of students' work from the previous year and build criteria together. "What makes this good?" Using their own vocabulary, the students talk about why "this is really good." And they come up with better suggestions for improvement every year. We model on an example of excellence from a previous year, or something that's out there in the real world. They know that these are the things we're working toward.

Then, the vocabulary is public. When I give comments on their drafts, or when they're working with peers on research, students ask me, "Do you think that this piece of information really shows insight into the character's development?" Students are looking at their research, and they're using the criteria in their discussions. It's extremely important to build the vocabulary early so they have a way to talk to each other.

Also important is modeling. We practice on me. I give my practice oral presentation, and I work in some good and some bad things. Then they practice giving me feedback. If someone says something I think is unsafe, I say, "Wait a second. Hold on. You just said something that makes me feel awful." So, it's me and they know that's okay. We practice. And if someone phrased something in a very excellent way, I stop—because remember, I'm teaching this skill. I say, "That was great. What did she do that was so good? What did she do?" And we have a discussion about how the feedback was phrased.

Working on feedback is a long process, but you try to be conscious of teaching this skill because you can't expect students to give each other good feedback right away.

Is a portfolio a documentation of personal growth and progress, or is it related to documenting an expedition? To what extent is it a reflection of individual student progress and achievement?

Eresh: Those are not separate questions, they're two sides of the same question. An expedition is supposed to teach me something about how I learn and how I grow, as well as about the subject matter. It's how much I get into the expedition, therefore how much I got out of it.

This notion of engagement is an incredibly important point that we need to remember all the time. It has to be the students' work that's meaningful and out of which it grows. And if the expedition can touch students, and students can be part of that and argue about it and fight about it and invest themselves in it, there's no difference between personal growth and the expedition itself. That's the end goal.

Greeley: This question made me think about the first time I sent portfolios home to the parents. I was totally focused on "This is a reflection of the work that you, the student, have been doing in the classroom. This is going to show your parents the growth that you've made and what you've learned," and so forth.

The day the portfolios went home, panic hit me because I realized, "This is going to show the parents what I've been doing in here." It was an incredibly vulnerable feeling because I don't use a textbook, and sometimes I feel very "out there" about what we're doing.

The portfolio is both. It is a real reflection of what students have done, and how they articulate their own learning. By the end of the year the portfolio is a map that documents where we have traveled together. And I think that's a reflection on the teacher, it's a reflection of the individual students,

and it's also a reflection of the classroom and all of the individuals in that classroom. My students' work is not just their footprints or mine, but the whole class', because they're constantly giving each other feedback and writing each other critiques. It's an ongoing process, and all of that emerges in the final portfolio.

> Working on feedback is a long process, but you try to be conscious of teaching this skill because you can't expect students to give each other good feedback right away.
>
> —Julie Craven

Craven: We're in a public institution and we're teaching not only what we think is important but what the community thinks is important too. When I look at portfolios from the public's perspective, it forces me to be very thoughtful about what I'm teaching. I have to know what it is the district wants me to teach, what I'm expected to teach, and I have to have thought about how I'm meeting those goals. So that it's not just "Oh, but the students are having fun." They should have fun, but they should also be struggling, learning, addressing issues, addressing what other people want them to explore.

This idea of accountability forces you to be thoughtful as a teacher, and it's extremely important. You can't just say, "Well, it's all about the students," because you can't separate the students from the community.

Brady: We need to be reminded that students can do good work. And we need to see it a lot to believe in it. The nation needs it now because there's a political climate where people are deciding, with good intentions, who is able to do good work. So I feel the purpose of our work is also political.

How can you encourage students to revise their work when they resist doing it?

Brady: Whenever I've done a field experience, I've never had a problem asking students to revise. They just love writing about an experience when they were out of the classroom.

Eresh: About ten years ago, I needed some students' work because I don't have students anymore. So I asked the teacher to give her students something to do, so I could have some papers to use in a training session.

She said, "Fine." But when I showed up looking for the papers, she threw them at me and was very angry. I said, "I'm sorry. What happened?" She said, "I told these students that this woman named Mrs. Eresh wanted some writing from them. And they went out, and they talked to each other. They brought it home, they got dictionaries, they had spellchecks, they wanted to use the computer. They spent all this time. They never did that for me."

It's the importance of audience and purpose. There's a lot of stuff that I should write and revise, but I have no real purpose in doing it. When I have a real purpose for doing it, though, when my boss says, "This report needs to be before the board next week," you can bet I'm going to spend Sunday revising it.

I think we have to give students reasons to revise their work. I think we have to give them some sort of audience, some sort of publication opportunities, and also acknowledge that not every piece is worth revising.

One of the techniques that's really simple is to have each of them do a lot of stuff in a writing workshop. And every three or four weeks you tell each to decide which piece he or she is going to take to publication. "Which one's worth working on?" So you give them some choices, and you give them some reasons for doing revisions. You know, you can "publish" anywhere. You put it in the hall. You can send it to the principal. Tell them you're sending it to somebody they don't know. There are all kinds of things. That can give them the motivation for revision.

Berger: Even if we, as teachers and administrators, are excited about the prospect of revision and think it's a sign of something good, that's not the way students usually see it. We all grew up feeling that if something came back for revision, it meant we did a poor job on it. And that's still the message that students tend to feel unless you change the game.

When a project is beginning, I'll even start by saying, "This is going to take a minimum of four drafts, but maybe fifteen." There are some projects where I don't even allow fewer than three or four drafts, and so getting back your work does not mean you did something wrong.

In fact, some students develop a perverse pride. If you visited my class they'd say, "I did fifteen drafts of this." The status is switched from "who got it right the first time" to "who took the most care with it."

Greeley: A lot of the time, students get things back to revise but they really don't know what to do with it. They don't know what's wrong with it. They just feel frustrated: "I have to do this over again?"

When the criteria are laid out for excellence in the beginning and the models are given, even then, you can have this model of excellence here and their work is over there, and the student is perplexed. And you say, "Well, let's take a look at it, really break it down and compare—look at what the criteria are and are we really meeting those things?"

Craven: Maybe this idea of revision is the core of portfolio culture. It doesn't just happen.

Look back at the revisions students have kept. How many of them are simply neatly copied over four times? Go back to draft one and compare it with the final draft. I would say the majority of students have changed almost nothing. Be honest with yourself: "Okay, look. This is what I'm trying to teach, strategies for revising. They're not revising."

If revising is extremely important to me, I'm really going to have to work through teaching revision. Don't be discouraged. You have to keep getting more and more conscious of it. That's the importance of having criteria, of going back and looking at them, perhaps building in Eliot Eisner's idea of "What's inspected gets expected," and "What gets counted counts."

I was playing with this idea and made it one of the things on my criteria and standard sheets. I told the students, "Revision is hard. I want you to rethink. Revision is not just rewriting it neatly. It's re-seeing it. So one of the things you're going to get graded on is your proficiency at revision." So if a student comes in at a high level and then shows no further advancement, she's going to get a "Satisfactory" or "Needs work" for revision. And a student who starts very low and really works at it, maybe she ends up at a much lower level in terms of the quality of the writing, but she's learned a lot about revision and made huge efforts. So she gets credit for that.

Something else that really struck me. There's a point where you look at a collection of work and divide it into "these students are ready for revision; these students still need instruction." This was a revelation for me. Revision requires that the students have an idea of the basic concept, and some students still don't get the concept. So I divide up the students sometimes. They're working with each other, they're revising, and some of them know the criteria and standard. And I say, "Okay, the rest of you come over here; we need to work on a couple of things." I still need to instruct them. And so it's grasping this idea that students can't revise until they've learned how to do it. But I think going back and looking at those drafts is a very good way to be honest with yourself. Are they revising, or are they just copying neatly nine times?

Greeley: It also means that you have to slow down. One of the questions we were posed was "What's been the toughest challenge for you in implementing portfolios?" The toughest thing for me has been slowing down and feeling like that's okay. Recall the story about the impatient man who is driving a friend to the train and keeps saying, "Come on, we've got to go, we've got to go get to the train. It's going to leave. It's going to leave." Well, the impatient man gets to the train station on time, only to discover that he has left his friend at home. Are we doing that with our children? Are we saying, "Come on, come on, come on, come on. We've got to get to the train," and leaving them all at home? This idea of revision means slowing down and asking students to do quality work rather than quantities of work.

Berger: I will defend the notion that it's valuable to set out a project, and say to the students right away, "There's no way you can do this in one draft." It takes a lot of pressure off the students. My students are designing homes right now, doing blueprints. And you can't design a home in one draft. Nobody can. Telling students, "There's no way to do this in one draft," slows them down and allows them to think. Maybe that's the lesson for all of us—we are building houses too; we need to remind ourselves as well, "Slow down, take time to think."

Parts of a Flower, by Jennifer Blow, a fourth-grade student at Clear Spring Elementary School in San Antonio.

What about grading?

Nathan: The way we're doing it doesn't make sense. It's broken. We really have to change the conversation. President Rudenstein of Harvard asked a group of teachers, "What could Harvard College do for education?" The resounding response was "Stop using the SATs."

Greeley: One of the things that portfolio work has done for me is just to force me to look at the criteria that I use for student progress. And I think that this is a huge, huge question. It's one that I have found myself getting lost in sometimes. What are we really assessing here? And what's the point of assessing? Am I supposed to be giving grades to give students feedback on how they've grown, or is this supposed to be helping students to become better learners? Is it supposed to be telling parents where their child stands in relation to other students, or where their child stands in relation to the parents' expectations?

The very first year I had a substantial portfolio really to look at, I had a grade form that I was sending home. And I had looked at the portfolios, and then I was filling in the grade forms. And I said, "These have nothing to do with each other." I mean, what I was grading students on—because I felt as if I had to—really wasn't at all a reflection of what had been going on in the classroom. And it was embarrassing. And then I asked the questions, "What's the purpose here?" and "Is this report reflecting the meaning of what we have been working on so hard in the classroom?" I redesigned my progress reports really to reflect the portfolio, and the portfolio is designed to reflect the structure of the classroom. We do give grades in our school because we think we have to. I really would like to see them abolished, and I don't think they're very constructive. But I think the idea of merit and feedback, and the criteria being clearly spelled out in the report card to the students is exciting.

But as I was using my new, more in-sync progress report one day, I would read the portfolio and then write the report. And I had left one student's portfolio at school, and I thought, "Well, I know this student. I'll just write this up." And I was stuck, I was totally stuck, because I knew the student but I really needed the evidence of the work to be able to get back into his thinking in a deep and meaningful way. And I just thought, "What have I been doing all these years before I started using portfolios to write the progress report?" So, I'm a real convert. I don't think they have to be in conflict with each other.

Berger: I think grades are ridiculous. To me, grades do nothing positive for students. Grades are useless for programmatic assessment, because they're entirely capricious. Schools set their own standards, and individual teachers set their own standards. It tells you nothing about a school to look at the grades in a school. So the only purpose of grades is to give students and parents feedback. And as probably many of you already feel, they're a very poor tool for giving students feedback. I think it makes students that are A students complacent. And it makes students that are C students stop trying. The grading system in my classroom is, it's A+ or it's not finished. If it's not their best work, it's not acceptable. And things just go back and back for revision.

Nathan: So what about the student who says, "I'm never going to be able to get an A." What happens to that student in your class?

Berger: Well, I spend a lot of time either by myself or with a colleague continually discussing, "Let's look at her work. How close is it to her best?" And we have to decide how much are we going to push it.

Nathan: So, is it okay if Kathy's best, for which she's getting an A+, is different from my best and my A+?

Berger: Absolutely. It's your best work that we're looking for.

Nathan: But I want my A+ to be different than Kathy's A+, because I'm a better student than Kathy. How do you deal with that?

Berger: Your best work is what's required of you. My feeling is that there's no key to teaching that gets away from the basic art of teaching. The basic art of teaching is, you get to know your students and you figure out how hard to push them. And you support them, but mainly you're pushing them in an encouraging way. And if you're a stronger student in that particular subject than Kathy in some way, I'm going to be pushing you a lot harder and expecting a lot more from you.

We've given no grades in our school for twenty years. And if we tried to institute grades now, there would be an uproar in the community. The people do not want grades; they love the fact that every student in the school feels as if he or she is a learner. No child in the town feels like, "I'm a D student." They love the fact that they learn more about their young people than people in neighboring towns. So, I'm again making an argument that there are a lot of reasons we're holding on to grades, but I'm not sure they are valid. I think parents in a way become an excuse for us to say, "Well, we could never abolish grades. The parents would never accept it." But I think once parents have changed over, they'll not want to go back.

Nathan: If we don't figure out a way to take this outside of our classrooms, it will never have a life of its own. But I think we need to take the long-term perspective. You have a responsibility in your classrooms to develop a system that makes sense to you. People talk about rubrics, and they talk about standards, and they talk about criteria. And you have a responsibility to develop these in your school and in your classroom, and that's the place to start—with your colleagues, and your school, and your school board, and your parents. ◆

Mieko Kamii is director of standards and assessment at Expeditionary Learning Outward Bound.

Looking at Student Work:

An Investigation into Alternative Assessment

Marie Keem, Arlene Agosto de Kane, and Marilú Alvarado

Expeditionary Learning's Design Principles—Self-Discovery, Wonderful Ideas, Success and Failure, Reflection—are the domain of teachers as well as students.

In January 1994, Arlene Agosto de Kane and Marilú Alvarado, fourth-grade teachers at the Rafael Hernandez School in Boston, sat down to plan a learning expedition. Inspired by the work done at Table Mound and Bryant elementary schools in Dubuque, Iowa, they decided to focus on pond life. In addition, they resolved to take on the challenge of exploring alternative forms of assessment. They asked, "What new or different form can assessment take so that we know more about how our students think and progress?"

Throughout the "Pond Life" expedition and the teachers' inquiry into assessment, a sense of the importance of careful observation prevailed. At the heart of the teachers' continued learning and professional growth was their willingness to challenge themselves to see, and then to let new sight and insight question their practice. Arlene and Marilú took the time to look systematically and carefully at student work. In terms of thinking about assessment as it relates to instruction and curriculum, they made three great strides in relation to instruction. The teachers began to examine student work and instructional situations, and asked the assessment questions "What do the students know?" and "How are the students thinking?" From there, they began to see assessment and instruction happening simultaneously.

Consequently, instructional goals evolved. In relation to curriculum, the teachers realized that the design of assessment activities has to be flexible enough to allow all students to express their knowledge. In other words, the mode of expression itself should not obscure students' content expertise.

Learning expeditions show that curriculum is most authentic and effective when it draws on the perspectives of multiple disciplines. This view of curriculum as a complex entity is best supported by

Yosenia Cabrera and Glenys Peña, middle-school students at the Rafael Hernandez School in Boston, compose at the computer. Photograph by David Cornwell.

a corresponding multilayered view of teaching and learning. Every moment of teaching and learning requires the lenses of both instruction and assessment. From this perspective, assessment is simultaneously knowing about individual progress—that is, knowing where a student is in relation to him- or herself—and knowing where that student is in relation to the potential of the material being explored. In this way, the dual viewpoints of instruction and assessment work in tandem.

Instruction and Assessment

I. Generating Profiles of Students' Learning and Thinking

In order to think about teaching and learning on a detailed and individual level, the teachers took on the task of looking very carefully and systematically at the work the students had produced. For example, the natural history journals in Arlene's class provided her with a substantial basis for delving into student thinking and identifying student progress. In these journals, students wrote their thoughts and impressions, recorded observations, answered questions from the teacher, drew creatures and plants at the pond, and wrote some of their own questions. The journals were not intended to be final products graded with an A, B, C, or D at the end of the year. Over time, they became tools for assessing student thinking, and as such they were tied directly to instruction.

Arlene's first step was to flip through several journals and think generally about what she had seen from reading and commenting on them periodically. Notes from the initial brainstorming session became a loose checklist that was her tool for generating a profile of each student's thinking and learning. This helped her come to know her students in greater depth.

The first section of the checklist described general work habits that were essential for student success throughout the year:

Responsible, careful, organized:

◆ Writes something when asked to
◆ Index to the journal is present
◆ Has original journal
◆ Is doing homework
◆ Takes notes from the board or in other appropriate situations (for example, muck sorting, pond activities)

The second section summarized elements that made up important skills and habits of thought throughout the expedition:

Observation, writing clarity, scientific method/thinking:

Observation—using two or more senses in combination for specific purposes such as: determining whether mixture of elements on display is dead or alive; identifying what a creature is; drawing; or writing.

Writing clarity—can someone else understand what the student has written and why she or he was writing? Can the student redraft writing so that it communicates his or her thinking better?

Scientific method/thinking—affective versus scientific interpretation ("I liked it, it was fun" versus "It stinks now and I think there's a creature in there but I can't see it"). Think about a continuum:

imagined	saw
affective response	scientific thinking

Since the scientific method was explicitly used by the class for certain experiments, it was important to see how much was reflected in students' journals. For example, "Are the various steps represented?" "Is there a connection between the question and the conclusion?"

By examining the journals systematically with the checklist in hand, Arlene was able to see many different elements in her students' work. For example, she noticed that one student went through a transformation from drawings that always had smiling faces to drawings that showed careful attention to detail.

In addition, from profiles and tallies of student work, Arlene was able to construct graphs that illustrated general trends in the students' ways of thinking and working. This in turn informed her sense of what to focus on in "Pond Life" the following year.

II. Assessment as Inquiry into Teaching

Marilú also engaged in a long process of inquiry regarding the way children learn to think scientifically. She started out wondering if the five-step scientific method (Question, Hypothesis, Experiment, Results, Conclusion) was too abstract for fourth graders. After trying to create icons (a question mark, a pair of eyeglasses, and so on) to help convey the idea behind each step, she went through a series of experiments in class. When she looked at the write-ups of those experiments closely, she realized that the teaching of the scientific method actually seemed to get in the way of scientific thinking.

Below are comments that one girl wrote in conjunction with a hay infusion experiment. For this, the students put pond water in a clear plastic cup and added grasses collected from the banks of the pond. They covered the cup with plastic wrap and made holes so that air could circulate, then let it sit to see what would happen. Following the scientific method, Marilú made sure the students wrote down questions and a hypothesis during the preparation stage. However, during the next step, it became clear that while the students were interested and were thinking a great deal, they were not connecting the experiment to their original questions and hypotheses.

QUESTION:
Will hay have insects in it?

HYPOTHESIS:
I think it won't because when the hay got insects it gets dry and they got out.

OBSERVATIONS:
Time: 1:03
Date: 4/7/94
Place: At the window
The hay looks ugly and it stinks and the hay is nasty.

Time: 1:09
Date: 4/25/94
1. The hay is growing green grass or algas.
2. Now I really think it is algas because the algas grows from the hay with a bunch of water.
3. Question: Will that hay infusion grow more algas? I think yes it will.

The two portions of the student's report represent two unrelated loops of reasoning and questioning. In the first, the student is heading into an unknown situation and tries to fulfill the first step of the scientific method—asking a question. So she puts down something general based on what comes to her mind when she thinks of ponds—insects. However, a more insightful question and hypothesis occur later on, after the student has been observing the hay infusion regularly.

After Marilú began this contemplation of scientific method, she invited a scientist friend into her classroom to do some simple experiments. He did several demonstrations regarding surface tension, but didn't call it that until the very end. At the same time, he engaged the students in a lengthy scientific discussion without referring to scientific method. As a result, Marilú's thinking took a new direction. She felt that in order for students to generate a question, she first had to give the children a chance to have an active experience.

> There were answers to the assessment question "What do the students know?" in everything they did.

◆ ◆ ◆

One of Marilú's goals for the next school year is to follow a different path to engage the students in scientific thinking. She will begin with hands-on work to spark the students' interest and foster questions about the material. Then she will lead students in going back and thinking about what they know and what kinds of clues they might already possess in answering their questions. After discussing their questions and what they know, the students will talk about testing their ideas and form groups to do that. The groups will carry out tests, make observations, report out, and reach a conclusion. Thus, Marilú has broken away from thinking of scientific reasoning as a lock-step method. Investigating, questioning, and hypothesizing are important themes that she will sound many times, in a flexible order, until the students reach conclusions. In this way, Marilú will

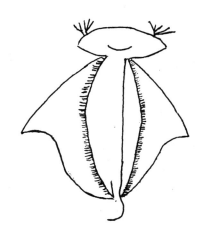

Three drawings by Dayanira Alicea, a fourth-grade student at the Rafael Hernandez School in Boston, for the learning expedition "Pond Life." The drawings show the progression of the student's observations over three months.

help the students develop the thinking strategies for being scientists.

III. Seizing Opportunities to Assess What Students Know

Claire Walker Leslie, a scientific illustrator who has written and illustrated several children's guides to pond life, visited Arlene's and Marilú's classes and led the children through several exercises that helped them become more comfortable with drawing. Eventually, this would help students depict the creatures and plants for their guides to Ward's Pond in Boston. For example, in the drawing of seashells, she asked the students to "try to see the shapes in your shells, they are basically variations on diamonds and triangles . . . " thereby adding a useful lens to the way they were perceiving their subjects.

The students had used Leslie's books as resources throughout the expedition, in particular one that described a pond as it looked at different points throughout the year. Here are some excerpts snatched from the enthusiastic exchanges that took place during the visit to Marilú's class:

CWL: Why is it important to date your journal entries?

Student A: For the teacher.

CWL: What if there was no teacher, why for yourself?

Student A: To know the season.

Leslie probed the student's thinking to see if there was further reasoning behind this certainty that journal entries must be dated. This conversation showed that the student understood one of the main ideas of the illustrator's book—that a pond looks different and has a different population at different times of the year.

Leslie also led the class through a number of student-directed sketches that surfaced student knowledge. For example, the students wanted to draw a painted turtle because one had been found and brought back to the school during a trip to the pond. In the process of drawing, the following exchange occurred:

CWL: Why is it called a painted turtle?

Student B: [Hesitates] . . . It's called painted because it looks painted.

Student C: It's painted yellow [points to the neck on the drawing] . . . and the shell is red or pink.

These types of responses demonstrate to the teacher that the students were combining observations and prior knowledge to make sense of the name assigned to the turtle. Through drawing and talking, students assimilated and anchored new knowledge and skills to an existing base. The conversations they had in the moment of learning exposed their insights and reasoning.

Marilú saw Claire Walker Leslie's visit as a new step in the curriculum, but she also realized that the students were revealing what they knew through the process of learning more. By actively observing what the students said, did, or assumed, the teacher could gain a sense of what knowledge and skills the children were building on or what misconceptions they had. There were answers to the assessment question "What do the students know?" in everything they did.

This kind of teacher-conducted observational assessment occurred in other ways as well. Both Arlene and Marilú asked their students to determine what they would write about the creatures and plants described in the two class field guides. Without prompts from the teachers, the students decided that they should discuss "habitat, metamorphosis or life cycle, food chain—who eats it and what does it eat?" in addition to other aspects, thereby showing that they had incorporated some of the major themes of the "Pond Life" expedition into their ways of knowing. In addition, Marilú and Arlene structured

> There are two aspects to a student's performance: the knowledge itself, and the mode in which the student is trying to express it.

◆ ◆ ◆

time for students to debate questions or observations. Rather than designing new assessments, the teachers saw that they could take advantage of assessment opportunities that were already in place.

By changing modes of assessment, teachers become researchers. But how can that role be integrated with the teacher's other roles in the classroom? Marilú wanted to record instances of what students said to build anecdotal records of progress for each member of the class, but she had to find a way to do it that would not take over every spare moment. Borrowing the ideas of Dubuque colleagues for an observation tool, Marilú thought of dividing a simple sheet of paper into 2-by-3-inch boxes for each student. On this sheet, she could

write observations about each student over a period of a few weeks. Over time, these entries would convey a sense of a student's growth.

The Evolution of Instructional Goals

When the teachers were planning an activity or looking back on one, they revisited the list of goals they had worked out during the planning stages of "Pond Life" to think about how these were coming together with instruction. This initial list of goals established a reference point for the teachers' thinking, but it also matured in important ways, both because the teachers themselves learned more about the pond and because they examined student work.

As the expedition progressed, Marilú and Arlene gained scientific knowledge that sharpened the vision that they later brought to the examination of student work. The teachers had begun the expedition with the close help of a science expert, Allison Mooney, who visited the school regularly from Wheelock College. However, throughout the expedition they were investigating and debating alongside the students and becoming content experts. As the three-and-a-half-month adventure progressed, Allison visited less and less. By the end, the teachers were thinking like scientists. That is, they were *in* the discipline as budding scientists themselves rather than teaching *about* it as outsiders.

As they gained content expertise and thought about how to assess student work, Arlene and Marilú began a second discussion of goals. It was much harder to set out a clear, concise statement with actual student trials, errors, and successes on hand. Out of the work rose nettlesome problems and questions—namely, how to bring together their knowledge of the strengths and weaknesses of their students and the exciting potential of studying pond life. Arlene began by looking for observational skills and scientific method/thinking in her students' journals. While examining her students' journals and final projects near the end of the expedition, Marilú decided that three checklists would be useful as observation organizers for next year, as shown in the box below.

In the later list, the content ideas came out organized according to major science themes. For example, observation subsumed drawing as a goal. Also, mapping was subordinated to the idea of habitats—establishing where certain creatures were

List of Goals from Planning Stage

Sorting, classifying
Observation skills
Graphing
Writing clarity
Data keeping, record keeping
Map skills, scaling
Key ecological concepts
Scientific Method, process
Environment
Estimation
Food chains
Life cycles
Drawings, models, observations

Marilú Alvarado's Later Lists

Skills:
Observing
Sorting
Hypothesizing
Experimenting
Investigating from secondary sources

Ideas:
Metamorphosis/life cycle
Food chain
Habitats

Attitudes:
Curiosity
Respect for living things

around the pond rather than topographical accuracy. Finally, the emphasis on hypothesizing and experimenting grew out of Marilú's examination of her students' experiments and her own thinking about scientific method.

Thinking about Curriculum and Assessment: Allowing Student Knowledge to Shine

When asking the question "What do the students know?" it is important to be clear-eyed about the fact that there are two aspects to a student's performance: the knowledge itself, and the mode in which the student is trying to express it. For example, asking a shy student to give a speech as a final presentation would put that student at a disad-

vantage for demonstrating his or her knowledge. Asking a student whose writing skills were developing more slowly than those of his or her peers to write an essay as a final assessment in a scientific subject would put that student at a disadvantage for conveying all that she or he might have grasped throughout an expedition. This is not to say that students should not learn how to write or that shy students should never be challenged to speak in public. Rather, at some point all students should also be given the opportunity to demonstrate their knowledge in the mode with which they are most comfortable.

Applying what they had learned about alternative assessment, Marilú and Arlene planned their final assessment for a "Marine Mammals" expedition. They remained interested in the students' scientific knowledge. An outline of their learning expedition and assessment plan follows:

◆ Dolphins and dogs actually have a common ancestor and some common features. For example, dolphins have five digits in their flippers.
◆ The evolutionary paths of dolphins and dogs from this common ancestor will be something the classes will study pretty closely.
◆ The students will be asked to consider another land mammal and invent a marine mammal that is linked to it via evolution, based on the dolphin-dog model.
◆ The students will create mock film strips (a paper roll through a box that they have designed) depicting the evolutionary steps between the land mammal and the marine mammal, and describing the anatomy and behaviors of the invented marine mammal.

The assessment will address the students' knowledge of evolution. Through the process of working from a land mammal and extrapolating their knowledge, students will consider the central question "What does it mean to be a marine mammal?" In addition, through the process of describing the invented marine mammal, the students will learn about the population of the sea. Success on this final assessment will not ride solely on the student's writing abilities. One student may write an essay; another could create captions and, in the form of an exhibition, narrate the "film strip" and answer questions from the audience without writing an essay—whatever it takes to express the student's thinking and knowledge as clearly as possible.

Teacher Laura Graves and student Billy Doyle, from Jack Elementary School in Portland, Maine, bake bread in class. Photograph by David Cornwell.

It is also important that students become more at ease presenting in modes with which they are not initially comfortable. In the case of "Pond Life," the final project was a field guide. Each student composed a page with an illustration and a short description, making sure to include certain details that the class had decided were important to know about each subject. Observing the students in class and at the pond revealed that all of them knew a lot and had developed good observation skills. The students were able to talk about many of the pond creatures, act them out, identify them in the pond, and draw at least rough sketches. Because the students so clearly knew a great deal, it was surprising that in the write-ups some copied the words from resource books. This made the teachers realize that summarizing skills would have to be a yearlong reading and writing theme for next year.

Marilú took pride in the fact that through the "Pond Life" expedition the students learned that they could consult books, each other, and other adults who came into the classroom. Perhaps most important, the students learned that a very important resource existed outside of the school—namely, the pond. One of Marilú's yearlong goals had been to have the children understand that they did not have to sit alone and do nothing if they did not have the resources to complete their work. A further step would be to have students learn to synthesize and reshape the information and opinions coming from the various sources that they consulted. In this way, they would be able to express their knowledge in writing when necessary.

Conclusion

Learning often takes the form of a spiral in which we consistently return to the same themes at increasing levels of sophistication. It is through such a pattern of revisitation that curriculum and assessment can be systematically reworked and improved. Examples of this process can be found in the Hernandez "Pond Life" study. When, at the end of the expedition, the teachers looked at the pieces their students had produced and thought about what constituted good work and good science, the goals of the expedition became more focused. The subsequent final assessment that the teachers designed for the "Marine Mammals" learning expedition drew directly on their experiences with "Pond Life." Perhaps most important, the teachers built a foundation for yearlong systems of assessment by thinking about specific tools they could create, delving into student thinking, and seeing assessment and instruction as different yet complementary opportunities in the same moment. ◆

Marie Keem was a research assistant at the Harvard PACE Project, and now lives and works in Paris, France. Arlene Agosto de Kane is a fourth-grade teacher at the Rafael Hernandez School in Boston. Marilú Alvarado formerly taught fourth grade at the Hernandez School, and currently is a doctoral student in Chicago who also consults with Expeditionary Learning Outward Bound.

Reading X Rays

Meg Campbell

I make this admission: initially I had difficulty becoming excited and deeply engaged in our work around portfolio assessment. I remembered a comment my daughter made to me once while she was struggling to make sense of a film we were watching. Adrienne observed, "It's not very interesting if you don't understand what's going on." Portfolio assessment was slippery and vague to me; I did not understand what was going on.

Dr. Mel Levine, director of Schools Attuned in Chapel Hill, North Carolina, tells a story about a conversation he had with a physics professor. Mel had asked the professor why, unlike the professor, he had not done well in physics, although he had done well in other science courses and had become a physician. "I probably had better metaphors than you did," the physics professor explained. "I was good at making those metaphorical connections between what I already knew and the physics I was learning."

Recalling Mel's story, I began to search for my own metaphor for portfolio assessment. I remembered as a child watching my father read X rays. I was amazed at how he could hold the black, gray, and white film of bones and tissue up to the light and pronounce that someone had a gallstone or a fracture. "Where?" I would ask. I could discern nothing. "There," he would reply, "see that tiny line?"—and he would guide my finger to a sliver of a shadow in a milky bone.

"You haven't learned what to look for yet, but you will. They'll teach you that in medical school. You get better at it. I'm much better now than when I started. And when I'm unsure, I ask one of my partners. I get a second opinion. So you don't have to know everything all the time."

Sitting recently with colleagues as we studied student work from a portfolio, I felt my time had come to learn to read X rays. Certainly I had evaluated, poked at, and analyzed student work before, but this time was different. Now I was look-

> Sitting recently with colleagues as we studied student work from a portfolio, I felt my time had come to learn to read X rays.

ing for where the growth spurts were as well as where the hairline fractures or dislocations might be. I was not working alone. I was soliciting second opinions. We kept referring back to the X ray before us. We kept looking harder and thinking harder about the student work. As we talked, we realized how easily our dialogue strayed off on tangents away from what we saw in the X ray. But when we disciplined ourselves to focus on the evidence before us, our findings were rich and useful.

We will improve at this new practice. My father, now seventy-two, is still reading X rays. When I am his age, I expect to be doing the same. ◆

Meg Campbell is the executive director of Expeditionary Learning Outward Bound, and codirector of the Harvard Outward Bound Project at the Harvard Graduate School of Education.

Building the Language of Critique

Kathy Greeley

For several years, I have emphasized to my students that writing is a process. We begin by brainstorming ideas or using some prompts, such as reading short excerpts that get the writing juices flowing. Students write first drafts and then bring them to peer "response groups" for feedback. They take the rich and thoughtful feedback they receive from their peers and rework their first drafts into richer, more thoughtful second drafts. Students then work in pairs or I read the next draft for another round of feedback. Again, the young writers return with insightful, useful comments for improving their work. Our last read focuses on spelling and mechanics. Students proudly turn in a final draft of polished writing. Right?

Wrong. While the above description is true to the philosophy of the writing process, what actually occurs in the classroom can fall far short of this vision. Teachers who have worked with young writers will have "smelled the rat" by the fourth line. The phrase "rich and thoughtful feedback" is a dead giveaway. In reality, students often give general, vague feedback that does not help the presenting writer. Comments like "I liked it" or "That was a good story" are common. Or, conversely, students focus on minute and often irrelevant details in an effort to make a concrete suggestion.

A few years ago at a conference at Harvard University, I saw Ron Berger present some architectural designs drawn by his sixth-grade class at Shutesbury Elementary School. When I first entered the room and saw them displayed on the walls, I assumed they were the work of graduate students from the Harvard Graduate School of Design. As Ron presented this outstanding work, he explained the important role of critique and revision in reaching such high stan-

dards. These students were not unusually gifted. Each of these extraordinary drawings resulted from several drafts of work. First, though, Ron pointed out, before students could effectively critique each other's work, they needed to know the *language* of architects. Every profession has its own special vocabulary that defines key elements of quality work. How did architects evaluate their design? What criteria did they use? What defines "good work" in a floor plan?

I realized that my students had not been able to give each other meaningful feedback on their work not because they were lazy or because they didn't care about improving their work, but because they lacked the language to do so. While I knew the elements of good writing, I had not clearly articulated them to my students. Asking students to analyze writing without giving them the vocabulary was like asking a carpenter to build a house without a saw.

Later that summer, I attended a workshop led by Linda Rief, who teaches eighth grade at Oyster River Middle School in New Hampshire and wrote the book *Teaching Diversity*. She presented an activity that I realized would help my students begin to build that technical vocabulary for writing. I decided to try it out that September.

At the workshop, Rief used six pieces of student writing from her classes which ranged widely in topic, genre, and quality. To maintain anonymity, I decided to use her students' work as samples (although one could use student writing from previous years). My students felt no ties to the writing or obligations to the authors. I handed out the first piece and read it aloud to students.

I then asked students to respond in writing to the following three questions:

1. What do you like about this writing (be specific about one thing—for example, a phrase used, use of dialogue, organization, and so forth)?
2. What is one question you would like to ask the author? (for example, can you tell me more about the mother? Or, where did you get the idea for this story?)
3. What is one suggestion you would make to the author for improvement?

Students did not need to write in full sentences but rather just jotted down notes that would trigger their memories for later discussion.

We repeated this exercise for the other five pieces. There was no discussion between each piece. Although this process of reading aloud and writing responses became a bit tedious for students, it forced them to listen carefully and to be specific about their responses to the piece.

After we read all six pieces aloud, students divided into small groups of four to six. I then asked them to rank the writing pieces from best to worst. I stipulated that they had to reach consensus on the ranking. Furthermore, they had to give a rationale and evidence for their choices.

◆ ◆ ◆

Asking students to analyze writing without giving them the vocabulary was like asking a carpenter to build a house without a saw.

◆ ◆ ◆

They dove into the task. Because none of the writings belonged to them, students saw each piece objectively and discussed each one freely. Given the range of quality in the writing, students easily sorted the first few pieces into two general camps: good writing and bad writing. But then it started to get tough. Some pieces had good qualities, but seemed to be missing something. I pushed them to rank each one in order, from best to worst, numbers one through six. I reminded them that their ranking would not be valid unless they had a clear explanation for their choices.

I started hearing some interesting discussions:

"I know this piece has some description, but it is *boring* description. 'The skis were 160 cm long. The brand of skis are Atomic.' So what?"

"I love how she compares the fish to a groundhog: 'I can see the tip of the fish's head over the side of the boat. It breaks through the water like a groundhog poking his nose through fresh, spring soil.' That is so great!"

"This poem really captures what it's like to go sledding. I love that line 'flying past white diamonds.'"

"I like how the writer used dialogue here, but I don't have a clue what they are talking about. 'Narly?' What's that mean?"

"I didn't get this poem at all."

"I didn't either, but I really like some of the lines."

"This piece doesn't go anywhere. What's the point?"

"I love this one because it reminds me of when I go to visit my grandparents."

Once each small group developed its ranked list, we convened again as a large group. I made two columns on a piece of newsprint of the elements we had discovered about good writing: what works and what doesn't work. As each group presented its ranking and rationales, I asked group members to articulate what we then could deduce about good writing. In explaining a low ranking, for example, one student said, "This piece just stopped; there was no ending. The author just left you hanging." I responded, "So that tells us that in good writing, we need to have closure, a clear ending."

Another student said, "I loved how the writer used lots of unusual comparisons to things, like comparing the setting sun to an orange."

"Does anyone know a special term for making comparisons like that?" I asked. We added *metaphor* and *simile* to the "what works" column.

As each group presented, our list of "what works" and "what doesn't work" grew. For example, good writing:

◆ Has real meaning and purpose
◆ Has a beginning, a middle, and an end
◆ Uses a strong lead to grab the reader's attention
◆ Is focused
◆ Has some structure
◆ Uses descriptive language
◆ Creates a picture in the reader's mind
◆ Uses dialogue to allow characters to speak for themselves
◆ Has rhythm
◆ Uses strong action words

We recognized that not every element on our list applied to every genre of writing. A poem may use repetition very effectively, but this may not be appropriate in an essay. The students liked the use of dialogue in personal narrative, but felt that it was not always necessary.

There was considerable disagreement about the "best" piece. Some students favored the poem about sledding, and others favored the personal narrative about the writer's grandfather. This stalemate created an opportunity to discuss personal taste and what makes the "best" writing: some of us love a piece because it reminds us of something in our own lives; sometimes we love a story because it opens our eyes to something new; some of us prefer science fiction to historical novels; some are confused by poetry. Students realized, though, that strong writing always has real meaning and purpose, and it connects to human experience in some way. They also realized that they could identify high-quality writing even if they were not personally drawn to the genre.

We did not exhaust the list of possible elements of good writing. However, we had developed, in our own language, a strong list of descriptors for students to draw from as they looked at their own and each other's writing. Students had identified for themselves at least twenty different criteria. We no longer had to settle for "I liked it." We had a tool, a working vocabulary that students had generated themselves by looking at actual work samples.

We no longer had to settle for "I liked it." We had a tool, a working vocabulary that students had generated themselves by looking at actual work samples.

I posted the list in the classroom and typed up a version for each student to keep in his or her writing folder. For the rest of the year, whenever students shared their writing drafts with each other, I asked them to get out their "Elements of Good Writing" list. We had these terms now; everyone had access to them. As students critiqued each other's work, I pushed them to give specific, concrete feedback.

When learning a new language, you begin by learning basic vocabulary. As a teacher, I tended to assume that students already had that vocabulary. While a few students did, most were unable to articulate easily their responses to other students' writing. However, many students discovered that they actually knew more about good writing than they thought they did. They just did not have the words for it. Learning those basic words was a key step in being more attentive readers and more attentive writers.

However, just learning the vocabulary is not enough either. We must ask students to use these words really to understand their meaning. One day, for example, after one writer read her draft aloud, I asked students to identify "what worked" in the piece. Rodney, with his "Elements" list in hand, offered a bit hesitantly, "She used descriptive language."

"Okay," I responded. "That's good, but now give us an example. Where do you hear descriptive language?"

Rocky Mountain School of Expeditionary Learning student Genevieve Akinwumiju studies bones during the "Human Body" expedition. Photograph by David Cornwell.

"Uhhh," Rodney looked sheepish. "I don't know." Other hands shot into the air.

"Try looking at the text again," I suggested.

"Well, I like how she described the rabbit," he said. "I get a good picture of what it looked like." Other students chimed in with other examples from the text, and together they showed evidence of the author's use of descriptive language.

This incident with Rodney reminded me of the importance of practice. We had created a powerful tool by constructing together our "Elements of Good Writing." However, I could not assume that all the students in the class felt adept at using that tool. We develop fluency when we use a new language frequently and in an authentic context. The same is true for our students. If we want them to be fluent in the language of writers (or musicians, or biologists, or sculptors, or mathematicians), we must give them frequent opportunities to develop, practice, and use that language. ◆

Kathy Greeley teaches middle-school humanities at the Graham and Parks School in Cambridge, Massachusetts and consults with Expeditionary Learning Outward Bound.

Cultural Divide

Mieko Kamii

Imagine a classroom in which teaching, learning, and assessment are thoroughly intertwined. Snagging the thread of assessment out of the fabric of teaching and learning would unravel the pedagogical tapestry of this classroom. Assessment serves teaching and learning in an ongoing fashion. Beliefs and practices linked with a "culture of assessment" have been established (see table on opposite page). In contrast, in traditional classrooms where the "culture of testing" reigns, learning and assessment are thought to be sequential activities: first you learn, then you assess (test). Separate post hoc assessment activities in the form of end-of-the-chapter tests and final exams are tacked on after the more critical and productive activities have occurred.

In the newer assessment culture, students look at models and exemplars of the things they are trying to produce before launching into their projects. If, for example, middle school students are sharing what they have learned about an ancient civilization by writing a storybook set in that time and place and intended for a younger audience of second or third graders, they look at examples of literature written for children of that age. They are given an opportunity to exchange ideas about what makes those works strong and appealing, ideas they can use to guide their decisions as they go about writing and illustrating their books. Teachers and students discuss criteria and standards explicitly and use them to assess student work.

Furthermore, students are encouraged to share their work-in-progress with the teacher and their fellow students. These members of the learning community give the student author feedback by offering their opinions about what is working well in the story and how the story or illustrations might be improved. The student can revise the work over time rather than turn in a first or second draft for a grade. The student thinks about her own and others' assessment of her work, and in this way assessment becomes an episode of learning.

In this example, assessment is embedded in the curriculum. The student uses and extends her knowledge in an authentic way by producing a storybook for another person, and that book—rather than a standardized test—provides the basis for assessment. The author is able to make her own connections between what she has learned most recently, and previously acquired knowledge, skills, and understandings.

In the assessment culture, results are public and shared rather than being kept private. The results are tangible rather than numerical and matter to someone beyond the self. The reason for privacy in the culture of testing is that assessment is fundamentally about ranking and sorting students. In turn, the practice of ranking and sorting is based upon the assumption that human abilities—most noteworthy among them "intelligence"—are distributed along a

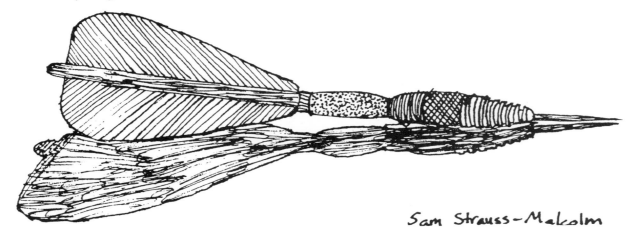

Line drawing of a dart by Sam Strauss-Malcolm, a seventh-grade student at King Middle School in Portland, Maine.

bell-shaped curve. Someone is always in the top, and someone is always in the bottom tenth, quarter, third, or half of the population. Percentiles and rank are emphasized rather than the content of what a student has actually learned or the quality of his work. By contrast, the point of assessment in the newer culture is to help students improve their performance and make progress toward meeting standards. Effort, hard work, perseverance, and a focus on high-quality work rule the day.

In the culture of testing, students (not teachers) learn and teachers (not students) assess. In classrooms, it is teachers who by virtue of their authority and expertise assess students. In large-scale achievement testing, testmakers and psychometricians dictate what teachers and students should know and the forms in which they should communicate their knowledge and understanding.

This is not so in the culture of assessment. In the classroom, peer assessment is central. Parents are also invited to become involved in assessing their children's behavior and work. Self-assessment and reflection are valued for the potentially powerful insights students can gain into their own strengths, weaknesses, passions, and preferences as learners. It can be argued that self-knowledge is no less important than "knowing that" or "knowing how," because the power to assess is linked to the power to decide, not only in classroom life but in the world beyond it. ◆

Mieko Kamii is director of standards and assessment for Expeditionary Learning Outward Bound.

As my high-school journalism teacher insistently reminded us, "Any news story worth printing must provide readers with answers to the w-questions: Who, What, Why, When, and Where." We borrow from her lesson to explain the difference between a classroom in which the "culture of testing" reigns, and one that has made the transition to the "culture of assessment."

—Mieko Kamii

Culture of Testing

What, When
- ◆ Exam, test, quiz.
- ◆ Post-hoc activity—assessment follows teaching and learning.
- ◆ One chance, one form.
- ◆ Tests items concealed.

- ◆ Results private.

- ◆ Curriculum distinct from assessment. "Teaching to the test" regarded as "cheating."
- ◆ Instruction distinct from assessment.

Why
- ◆ Ranking, sorting.

- ◆ Presumption that abilities are distributed along a bell-shaped curve.

Who
- ◆ Distant experts, authorities dictate test content; teachers merely administer tests (ITBS, CATs, SATs).

Where
- ◆ In a chair—"quiet, no talking."

Culture of Assessment

- ◆ Ongoing and culminating activities,
- ◆ Feedback on work-in-progress; asking questions, listening to critique sessions, etc.
- ◆ Drafts, revision over time.
- ◆ Public process; standards and criteria known in advance; models, exemplars provided.
- ◆ Work products and performances public (exhibitions, performances).
- ◆ Assessment embedded in the curriculum; curriculum and assessment are joined.
- ◆ Assessment becomes an episode of learning; teaching and assessment are joined.

- ◆ Supporting teaching and learning; focus on improvement, progress toward meeting standards.
- ◆ Presumption that effort, hard work, and perseverance count.

- ◆ Teachers, peers, self, and parents participate in assessment.

- ◆ In a chair, on the stage, indoors, outdoors, school, home, wherever a good idea can be found.

Part Four

Taking Risks: Linking the Wilderness to the Classroom

When I [first] read the design principles, I thought, "Oh, I'm already doing this." Now that I've been on an Outward Bound course, I feel I have lived the design principles. They are internalized. Before, they were just words on paper.

—Anita Dorsey, instructional facilitator

Springdale Elementary School

Memphis

Leaving the Ledge

Kathy Greeley and Amy Mednick

This article is in part based on the journal entries of Amy Mednick and Kathy Greeley.

In the morning, we ate Grapenuts and didn't even boil water for tea. We packed up our "Mel" bags, a stuff sack converted into a backpack, and headed for a day of rock climbing.

Once at the rock, I was awed by its height and steepness. My heart beat rapidly when I entered the "helmet zone." I wasn't sure if I could muster the courage to try. But then, I didn't think I could carry the backpack either.

So, I volunteered to climb first up a route that would take me two-thirds of the way up the rockface. Later, I found out that that represented one hundred feet.

Matt's lesson during belay school helped because I focused on "finesse" rather than on trying to "haul" my way up the rock. I also took his word that sticking out your butt and relying on your legs more than your arms would help. Something clicked. I trusted myself.

I made it about ten feet up, and I was stuck.

Matt said, "Come on Amy. You just danced up that rock. What are you waiting for?" He pointed out that I felt really comfortable resting on the small ledge, and that the security was hard to give up. Those words of advice helped me maneuver past the ledge. I struck up the nerve and ventured up the white streak of rock Matt said would have lots of small ridges. It was as though it wasn't me. I was being led by some inner driving force.

A novice climber freezes when steadied by the comfort of a small ledge. In the same vein, educators hesitate to leave the comfort zone of their lesson plans, classrooms, and school. As educators begin to change their practice, to try teaching in new ways, they often feel that fear of stepping out from the safety of the ledge. Yet the trust in oneself expands exponentially when one makes it to that next foothold.

Over the past three years, Expeditionary Learning Outward Bound has invited many educators, teachers, principals, professors, and superintendents on Outward Bound courses to deepen their understanding of our philosophy of learning.

In August, as part of the New American Schools invitational for new Expeditionary Learning jurisdictions, nine women educators set off on a North Carolina Outward Bound School course into the Pisgah National Forest in North Carolina. Memphis principal Cherrie Wondemagegnehu asked repeatedly as we trudged up muddy trails through rainstorms in our Helly-Hanson raingear lugging fifty-pound backpacks, "What does this have to

A Rocky Mountain School of Expeditionary Learning (Denver) student makes his way up the ropes course. Photograph by David Cornwell.

do with Johnny learning to read?" From our instructors, Trina Abbott and Diana Belknap, of the North Carolina Outward Bound School, there were no direct answers. It was up to Cherrie, and our crew, to figure that out.

I hated giving up my watch. I hated never being told what we were going to do. I felt so disempowered.

From the beginning of the trip, Trina and Diana encouraged the crew to live in the present, rather than to anticipate next steps. They collected watches, and deflected questions about what was to

◆ ◆ ◆

As in a classroom, our group was mixed heterogeneously, coming from diverse backgrounds with a range of skills, experience, and comfort in the woods.

◆ ◆ ◆

come. For a group of educators, who were used to being in charge, this was difficult. The issue of control is key to teachers. Teachers want to be prepared. They want to know what they will cover each day and what important questions they will ask. Teachers are held accountable for covering certain skills and bodies of knowledge. But sometimes, when teachers are willing to set a course without knowing every detail of the journey, their discoveries can be profound. When they allow new revelations to seep through the cracks of habit, learning can become alive and vibrant and deep.

Juanita prepared to head up a shorter but more difficult climb. As she started up I was struck by her perseverance, strength of soul, and willingness to exert herself. Grunting and panting, she inched her way up, with the rest of us calling encouraging hints and ideas from below. After Kim lowered her down, Juanita was crying, I was crying, Kim was crying because the experience was so powerful. Held fast by her future colleague, Kim, Juanita said she felt secure. It's a bond that won't fade.

Throughout the course, as the crew met new challenges, there was a reservoir of support, caring, and trust for each individual to draw on when she needed extra strength. Without the nurturing of the group, Cherrie said that she could not have managed the heavy backpack, steep trails, and hard ground. As a principal, Cherrie is committed to transporting those intense relationships to the school, among staff and children. "If every teacher would provide this type of support and care for not just the children but also fellow team members, it would have everybody learning because everybody would feel successful."

On the trail each individual wrestled with the fear of failure and the determination to succeed. As in a classroom, our group was mixed heterogeneously, coming from diverse backgrounds with a range of skills, experience, and comfort in the woods. Despite the differences, at the outset the group was committed to sticking together, resolved that everyone would succeed.

I was interrupted by an intense lightning storm. First I thought it was a plane in the distance, but when I realized it was thunder I went to my tarp and crouched on the insulated pad scared out of my wits. . . . When the storm let up I ran back to the main campsite. Trina and Diana calmed me down and helped me relocate. . . . I felt like I had failed my "solo" and dreaded the next morning.

When the crew gathered for a final breakfast to share their stories of the twenty-four-hour solo, Amy described her panicked decision to seek help from the instructors during the storm. As she lamented her seeming failure, Amy's crewmates challenged her to reassess the experience.

"It depends on your definition of success and failure," Kathy said. "By asking for help you got the support you needed to make it through the night, and that was your goal."

"It was like climbing that rockface," said Janet Weingartner, principal of Midway School in Cincinnati, Ohio. "When you couldn't move forward you moved laterally, and then started up again. It's the same with our children." The circle of women continued to reflect on bringing back to the classroom new meanings of success and failure.

"For me personally," Cherrie later said, "it was a lot of success and a lot of failure. Many times I felt I had failed when I slowed the group down because I would get tired. I felt I was the 'special education kid' in the group, but each time I was assured some success so that gave me the spirit to keep going." Asking for help, needing extra support or instruction, making a lateral move across the rockface are all valid steps that help students ultimately reach their goal.

I set to work setting up my tarp. I tried using sticks for stakes, kept adjusting the height of the two tarp lines, tried finding "tent poles." I remembered the sliding knot, and I finally got a good tight stretch on all four corners with a good slant for drain-off. I was so pleased with myself. I wanted it to rain so I could test it out.

To succeed in the woods the crew learned skills necessary to survive. Diana and Trina taught the essential knots to erect a tarp the first night, and then the crew pitched the tarps for the rest of the trip. If the group did not tie knots correctly, rain would get the tarp and sleeping bags wet. In order to make it from one campsite to another, the instructors taught the group to use a map and compass. If the group came to a fork in the trail, the crew knew it was time to figure out the answer to the unspoken question on its own. Learning related directly to real-life success. While teachers and students might not find themselves out in the woods, their learning also needs to have purpose and direct application to real-life experience.

The solo was a profound experience for me. The solitude was difficult at first, but in the end it was like loosening a knot. All sorts of thoughts, feelings, observations were allowed to pass through. I'm very intrigued with how we can create that time and space in our everyday school lives.

In the evenings after dinner, the crew would circle up and reflect on the day's events, whether it was hauling backpacks in the rain or struggling up a steep hill. In the safety of the campsite, people found lessons in what initially seemed just another arduous task set before them. Without this chance to reflect with the group, Amy would have felt she had failed her solo. Instead, it became a true learning experience, and memories linger of the friendly hummingbird by the stream, rather than the frightening storm.

By the end, everyone agreed that schools should find a way to build into the day both personal and collaborative reflection. "A person needs to stop and think about what I did, what I didn't do, and what I would do differently," said Anita Dorsey, the new Expeditionary Learning facilitator for Springdale Magnet Elementary School in Memphis. "I do that with my children in school." Through this process, children make sense of their own learning.

After a great dinner last night, we sat outside in the grass overlooking the city of Asheville with the mountains in silhouette behind. We sat and talked about the ten Expeditionary Learning Outward Bound design principles—each of us being the "steward" of one of them.

Cherrie's question "What does this have to do with Johnny learning to read?" still had not been answered directly. But, as the best teachers do, our instructors had posed challenging tasks, given us the skills to accomplish them, had encouraged us to draw on both our individual and our collective knowledge, and patiently allowed us to make our own discoveries. Little by little, we experienced the meaning of the design principles. As we gathered one last time for a conversation about the expedition, Cherrie practically jumped out of her seat: "I get it! I get it now!"

The Natural World

In this illustration, sixth-grade student Caroline Lundberg, of Bryant Elementary School in Dubuque, Iowa, interprets the Expeditionary Learning design principle The Natural World.

Expeditionary Learning school designer Scott Gill leads a group of Dubuque teachers in a team-building activity. Photograph by David Guralnick.

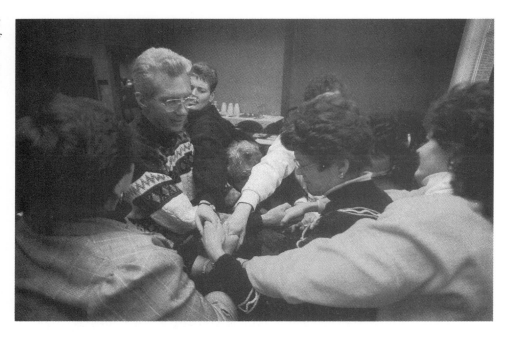

As each educator shared her thoughts about the design principles, about her own learning, and about how to bring that back to her students and colleagues, the group members recognized that they had discovered a deeper meaning in the design principles. Perhaps Anita captured it best in a conversation after returning home from the Blue Ridge: "When I [first] read the design principles, I thought, 'Oh, I'm already doing this.' Now that I've been on an Outward Bound course, I feel I have lived the design principles. They are internalized. Before they were just words on paper."

While the circle of women realized this collectively, each individual also came away with a distinct self-discovery that resonated with her own personal experience. Cindy Winburn, physical education teacher at Midway School, was inspired constantly to set up learning environments that challenge the students to accomplish more than they think they are capable of achieving. For Judy Wahl, a math teacher at Peoples Middle School in Cincinnati, Ohio, the opportunity to "have wonderful ideas" enabled her to stay dry during her solo. For everybody, these five days had been an expedition into purposeful, profound learning.

I think if we can sometimes loosen our grip we can allow a different voice in ourselves, in our teaching, to breathe. I think about the design principle of "The Having of Wonderful Ideas." As I let go of needing to know our trip's agenda each day, I opened myself up to a whole other level of observation, feeling, and awareness. That freed me up to admire the rays of sunlight on a wet rhododendron leaf. ◆

Kathy Greeley teaches middle-school humanities at the Graham and Parks School in Cambridge, Massachusetts and consults with Expeditionary Learning Outward Bound. Amy Mednick is the editor of The Web.

Courage of Learners

Deb Otto

Dropping out of the sky, the pilot points to a trail tracing a path across a Colorado ridge. "This is it!" he exclaims as he rudders left and guides the nose of the plane until it aligns with a narrow road. A green car speeds along the gravel lane, leaving a trail of dust behind, and I wonder just what I am in for on this trip. The flight from Salt Lake City to this remote location has been breathtaking and stomach wrenching as the seven-seat plane navigated over the Uinta Mountains. We are grateful to touch down and enjoy watching the other three planeloads of educators, headed on the same Outward Bound invitational course, land successfully. The pilot throws the gear out of the storage bays and onto the roadside. Our pilot says we can hang around until someone comes for us, or start walking "thataway." Eager to be active members of the much-awaited river-rafting expedition, we walk.

After a night sleeping under a tarp among snoring crew members, I wake to a 34-degree August morning. The day promises sunshine warmth and delivers it on time as our rafts are pumped up, loaded, and made ready to go. Finally, I board the *Tempest* raft alongside my seven crew members, and with three other rafts and crew, begin our journey down the Green River in Dinosaur National Monument. During the next few days this band of strangers will become a competent crew as we scout and run the rapids from the Canyon of Lodore in Colorado to Split Canyon in Utah.

The directions from Jeff Jackson, our Outward Bound instructor from the Colorado Outward Bound School, seem simple enough: forward, back paddle, left turn, right turn, and relax. We will each take a turn as captain, learning to guide the boat from the rear with draw and pry strokes that set the direction for the paddlers. The job of captain looks easy

enough but when tried is "counterinstinctive," according to one crew member, and takes some practice.

This learning feels very different from my norm, a little uncomfortable, even shaky at first. Usually a quick study in all school-related business, I am not sure I like this uncertainty and dread my first captaining of the boat. Inevitably, my turn begins as we approach "Hell's Half Mile." For each set of rapids we drag the rafts ashore and walk the length of the rapids, looking for the best path, locating markers and obstacles. Then we scramble back to the rafts and prepare to navigate the waters. For "Hell's Half Mile" we determine that our guide will captain and I will take over just after. It looks so easy for him. However, when it is my turn my instincts fail me, and in the flattest of waters, we hit the canyon wall and snag on a "sleeper," a slimy,

Athena Hom, a student at School for the Physical City in New York, reflects in her journal on her experience in a sweat lodge built of birch during an expedition at Camp Minisink. Photograph by David Cornwell.

moss-covered rock hidden just below the surface. After much trial and error, the raft begins to go the way I intend and captaining improves, meaning we miss more rocks than we hit. Near the end of my turn as pilot, the *Tempest* is dubbed the "Rock Magnet," and the crew now excels at dislodging our craft.

◆ ◆ ◆

Without the river, a raft, and a teacher who understands the importance of self-discovery, I would not have a rejuvenated perspective on the courage of learners.

◆ ◆ ◆

Reflecting on the day's journey during our overnight solo, alone in the woods, those feelings of uncertainty and the struggle to develop a captain's skills nag at me. These must be the emotions students in my school feel every day. In fact, I must have felt them again and again in my own schooling, but I had forgotten what they were like. Every day we ask our students to take risks such as exposing weaknesses, failing to perform well, looking stupid in front of others, and making errors. How lucky I am to restore that feeling in myself: I feel fortunate to be set back a notch or two in my own learning even though that experience can be painful. It allows me a clearer understanding of how much some children struggle with learning. The support of the crew and patience of the instructor have allowed me to shed the need to be correct and safe. Without the river, a raft, and a teacher who understands the importance of self-discovery, I would not have a rejuvenated perspective on the courage of learners.

Of course, the trip ends too soon, just as it begins to feel good to be dirty, when dry feet are

Student Devon Hencmann balances himself atop a hanging beam on the ropes course at the Rocky Mountain School of Expeditionary Learning in Denver. Photograph by David Cornwell.

the reward for a day's work, when digging deep with the paddle becomes a welcome rhythm. The memories of the trip are with me: scenery beyond description, sounds of the rapids, talk among new friends, the night sky, shared fun. But these are the common memories, similar to those from any vacation or family outing. My renewal as a learner is the real treasure I discovered in the canyon. ◆

Deb Otto is the principal of Lincoln Elementary School, an Expeditionary Learning Outward Bound demonstration school in Dubuque, Iowa.

The World of Ice, Snow, Skis, and Dogs

Kathy Witherup

S mall white dots filled every inch of the sky. The Big Dipper, Hercules, Andromeda, and other constellations popped out of the dark night. The moon shone brightly. It was 32 degrees below zero, and I felt the chill in my toes and fingers. I wondered if my eyeballs would freeze.

Expeditionary Learning school designer Scott Gill takes a turn leading the dog team on the Voyageur Outward Bound educators' expedition in the Northwoods of Minnesota. Photograph by Kristine Mosher.

I lay on the ice on Little Gabbro Lake in the Northwoods of Minnesota double zipped inside two mummy sleeping bags with only my eyes exposed to the glacial air. It was the second night of the Dog Sledding Educator Invitational with two instructors from the Voyageur Outward Bound School and five other educators from the Expeditionary Learning Outward Bound network. On one hand, my companions and I fretted through the night about our exposure to the extreme cold. On the other hand, we were glad to experience the wonder of the night sky.

It had been a hard day traveling with a backpack, and trying to ski with what felt like two slippery boards on my feet. But our mixed-aged group, ranging from the early twenties to sixty years old, was very attuned and observant of each other's needs, strengths, and weaknesses. We knew within an hour who was struggling, who was comfortable, who was experienced, and who needed help. As we embarked on the first portage—a departure from the smooth, snowy lake to the more strenuous steep land—my supervisor and longtime colleague Kathleen Ware struggled to keep up. She bent over her skis, breath-

◆ ◆ ◆

The moon shone brightly. It was 32 degrees below zero, and I felt the chill in my toes and fingers. I wondered if my eyeballs would freeze.

◆ ◆ ◆

ing deeply. We stopped so that she could mush— drive the dog sled—instead of ski up the hill. As Kathleen, a lead administrator in Cincinnati, said later, "It was mush or death for me. I had to get that pack off my back."

Skiing on ice and on narrow passages with bushes, twigs, trees, and deeper snow are two extremely different experiences. The hills were hard to negotiate while hauling a forty-pound backpack and trying to ski on two "planks." As I skied along, questions arose: When you fall, how do you get up? How do you get the skis in a herringbone pattern without getting a twig or bush caught up in them? How do you keep your balance so that you do not

Rafael Hernandez (Boston) middle school students push a cart carrying their camping gear on an expedition at the Thompson Island Outward Bound Education center.

topple over? As a group, however, we went forth with the confidence that we could make it. Those who were more experienced showed and demonstrated a "climbing" process to those of us new to skiing. Frustration set in for some of us, while other crew members exhibited patience, support, and encouragement.

During the expedition it was too cold to write down my thoughts. But snowed in afterward in a warm Duluth hotel room, I curled up with a pillow and reflected on the adventure. I thought about my own challenges and their applications to the classroom.

A Time for Questioning

Cross-country skiing in single file gave me time to think and reflect. For the first time, I experienced the type of person I am when things get really tough. I began to talk to myself and ask questions: Am I a quitter? Am I a fighter? Am I a complainer? Do I

retain my humor? Can I adjust? Am I flexible? Am I rigid? Do I change my approach and method so I can still accomplish the goal? Am I a loner and do I go off and do my own thing? Do I stay by myself? Do I encourage and help others? These are hard questions and realizations when you are in a foreign environment and do not know your fellow travelers. It is so different from the safety of a classroom.

◆ ◆ ◆

These are hard questions and realizations when you are in a foreign environment and do not know your fellow travelers. It is so different from the safety of a classroom.

◆ ◆ ◆

The crew entered a flat sheltered bay on a lake. We had skied most of the daylight hours. My companions and I were not aware of time, but we were aware of the growing darkness. We were tired. But there was no camp yet. We wondered: What do we do now? Who does what? Where do we begin? I looked around and I saw a ski pole "farm" we had created with backpacks strewn across the flat icy area! It was really laughable to see these "modern conveniences" in a world of snow, ice, trees, and whiteness. They looked out of place.

Kirstan Dally, our instructor, took charge. She described what needed to be done, and people began volunteering for jobs. It was getting dark, and the temperature began to drop. We became efficient worker bees buzzing around gathering wood, chopping wood, sawing wood, hauling wood, emptying the sled, caring for dogs, and putting up the wall tent where we lit the stove and ate dinner. We cleared an area for the sleeping tarps, and dug holes for "zombies," scraps of wood used as "stakes" to keep the tarp from blowing away. So many tasks. Head lights went on. Additional clothing was layered so the cold could not penetrate. No longer were we individuals, or a group; we were a team. We had a purpose, a goal, a desire.

The jobs were completed. We laid our insulated pads on the ice and placed our sleeping bags on top of them. Our little, open-air home looked wonderful.

There was a sense of relief that we had finished the major work for the day. We were hungry and tired. We headed for the wall tent to engage in conversation, eat our food, and dry our clothes. The wall tent was warm with heat, good cheer, and a feeling of camaraderie. We sat on the snow benches and formed a circle in the Outward Bound tradition.

It was a day to experience success and failure. Once warm, Kathleen said, "I've never been a failure at anything before. School was always easy. My job is always a challenge, but I am always successful. However, today I felt failure. I couldn't keep up with the group. I was holding everyone else back. My back was killing me. I thought I was in better physical condition than I am. The only success I had was taking Buster, the sled dog, to his picket line. I'll always be thankful for Buster—he saved my self-esteem today."

The group reflected, modified plans, and redefined how our team would work. Then eyes began to close and yawns were heard. People began to get things together to venture out into the cold, dark night. I questioned my sanity for taking on this challenge. It was 32 degrees below zero. I had to get in my two mummy sleeping bags. We mustered the strength and courage, and ran into the night. Once inside the mummy bags with feet and hands tingling as they warmed up, I thanked myself for accomplishing the little things—a zipper, a snap, a belt, drinking the brown water, and not losing a glove or hat. It had only been one day. But I had accomplished so much already. I said goodnight to the others and listened to the wind blow in the open expanse of the Northwoods.

Bringing the Challenge Home

Throughout the entire trip I kept relating what I was learning to the education of children. There were many comparisons, and I am thankful that Cincinnati has begun implementing educational reform efforts that will benefit the whole child, including dimensions of self-esteem, intellect, social interaction, and emotional well-being. It is wonderful to have Expeditionary Learning Outward Bound as one of our New American Schools designs. Expeditionary Learning's design principles match our reform efforts. I took home four major lessons from this challenge.

◆ Be aware of others' needs. As I struggled to put up the tarp, I kept thinking of our students and how hard it is for them to enter a classroom in the fall when they do not know their classmates, their teacher, or the building, and they are unfamiliar with the rules, regulations, and expectations. They experience the same fears and concerns that I did on the course. How does the teacher react? It is a "portage" for both the teacher and the student. It is almost life threatening—learning or death. They can succeed or fail. What will the teacher do to ensure some success each day?

◆ Concentrate on the simple, little things. Our instructor Kirstan reminded us at our evening Outward Bound "circle up" that all of us in the group were task-oriented people, and we were accustomed to completing a task. But on this expedition we had to take care of the little things. Cold hands and feet could result in frostbite or worse. Therefore, we had to take care of those details before we completed a task.

Sometimes it is necessary to stop a task and not complete it if other, more important issues emerge. The same is true for teachers. We get so concerned about covering the curriculum that we forget to help our children learn or experience the small steps, a necessary lesson, or the relevance an adventure on the playground has to class time. We must take the time to look around and enjoy and learn from the little things.

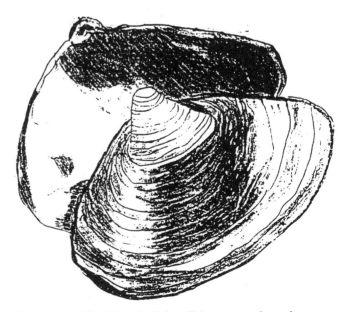

Illustration of Surf Clam by Robert Price, a seventh-grade student at King Middle School in Portland Maine, for the Casco Bay learning expedition.

Circumference - 1.13 inches

Artwork by Cal Follman, a student at Central Alternative High School in Dubuque, Iowa, for the "Natural Reflections" learning expedition.

◆ Be observant and give support to those who need it. Kirstan and Bob Schultz, our other instructor, were observant of our behaviors, strengths, and weaknesses, and they listened to what we said and how we said it. They actually heard us. They did not always sympathize with us, but they did empathize with us. They also knew the trail and what was around the next corner, and gave the appropriate encouragement and support, asked the right questions, or suggested different ways to accomplish the task. Not all six students achieved the goal the same way, but each of us did accomplish the goal. It is this observing, knowing, and suggesting that makes the best teachers.

I was afraid to go down one of the hills on a portage. I was struck with fear that my skis would fly down and I would fall again. I began to go down in the deeper snow. A mistake. But Kirstan guided me back onto the path and talked me into using my ski poles as brakes to get down the steeper part of the hill. Once I accomplished that, she encouraged me to let go and ski down the hill.

It worked. I did it, and everyone clapped. Without that gentle prodding and guidance, I would not have made it. She did not accept failure, but she did accept using a different method to assuage my frustration.

Educators must look out each minute for a student who needs that guidance, support, prodding, and suggestion of a "different" alternative method in order to feel confident enough to go on and accomplish the goal. A little success goes a long way.

◆ The team is vital to survival and accomplishment of the goal. Although my crewmates and I were diverse in experience, age, skill, background, intellect, and knowledge, we each had skills the others did not. By relying on each other, the group members together accomplished the goal of finishing the course. We carried packs for each other. We assisted each other with zippers and belts. We helped saw and chop wood. We talked each other through difficult times and ate gorp together. We laughed and complained together. We were concerned for each other, and we wanted each other to succeed. If one person had not completed the goal, everyone in the group would have suffered and everyone would have been responsible. Teamwork was vital.

As an administrator in Cincinnati Public Schools working with teachers to reform the educational practices in the classroom, I found that the valuable lessons learned on this expedition can be applied to my job as manager of new programs. This was the hardest physical challenge I had ever encountered in my life. Teachers are experiencing educational challenges every day in the classroom. So, I must remember that teachers and principals will implement the reforms, but not in the same time frame or in the same way. Changing the way we instruct students is just as hard as skiing up a hill lined with bushes. Many teachers will need extra support and much encouragement. I must be observant and understanding, and give guidance when frustration or struggling occurs. Small successes will foster other successes. I must be patient. Teachers must feel confident and successful to continue to try. If these lessons can be followed, reform will take hold in Cincinnati. ◆

Kathy Witherup is a Cincinnati Public Schools administrator working with teachers and principals to implement school reform policies and designs.

Peak Performance

Susan Black

What's the link between mountain climbing and education? Advocates of Expeditionary Learning are finding out.

Lewis and Clark headed west. Admiral Richard Byrd went to the North Pole. Sir Edmund Hillary trekked to the top of the world in his ascent of Mount Everest.

A more down-to-earth kind of discovery—but one that captures the spirit of these explorers and others—is at the heart of Expeditionary Learning Outward Bound, an enterprise based in Cambridge, Massachusetts, that's lining up students, teachers, school executives, parents, and community residents to experiment with new ways of teaching and learning.

Since adopting the Expeditionary Learning design, schools in five cities (Boston, Denver, New York City, Dubuque, Iowa, and Portland, Maine) are reporting success on two major goals: aiding students' intellectual growth and their character development. And there are encouraging signs, reported in an independent audit of the program published by the Academy for Educational Development in New York City. According to the study, both "transformed schools" (schools that have switched from traditional programs to the expedition model) and "phased-in" schools (new schools founded on the principles of Expeditionary Learning but just beginning to set the principles in motion) are gaining ground on the three concepts that guide Expeditionary Learning. Those concepts are: (1) placing learning and character development together at the pinnacle of a school's values; (2) requiring all students to demonstrate character development and academic achievement at critical points (third, eighth, and twelfth grades) in their schooling; and (3) organizing a school's resources (such as staff, classrooms, schedules, and instructional materials) to support students' learning.

In the eleven pilot schools committed to the Expeditionary Learning design, teachers are guiding students through expeditions—"journeys into the unknown"—where they explore topics through their own questions and self-styled investigations. In

---

Wood duck drawing by Willie Thoma, a fifth grader at Table Mound Elementary School in Dubuque, Iowa, for the learning expedition "Do You See What I See?"

Boston, for instance, middle schoolers are involved in a semester-long study of the Industrial Revolution called "Wheels of Change," while in Dubuque's Table Mound Elementary School, fifth graders examine pond life under microscopes in a two-month study called "Do You See What I See?"

"It's a tremendous amount of work," says a teacher who's leading her energetic middle schoolers through the process. "But seeing the wonder in my students' eyes when they present their original research and their own products makes the effort worth it." And how do students feel about their journeys? Fifth grader Dallas Kalmes writes in his journal: "I felt like a real scientist looking into a microscope, and when I found the specimen, I felt awesome. It's like you wrote a new chapter in the encyclopedia. Six weeks ago, I never would have known about pond life."

Credit for funding these eleven Expeditionary Learning schools goes to the New American Schools Development Corporation (NASDC), a private non-profit group founded during the Bush administration as the research and development arm of the school reform movement and currently supported by the Clinton administration. The group's goal: to fund "break the mold" school designs that can be replicated across the country. Expeditionary Learning Outward Bound is one of nine proposals NASDC accepted to receive five years of financial support; when the current funding cycle ends, each of the nine models will begin a two-year phase of dissemination and replication so other schools can adopt their designs.

For now, though, getting Expeditionary Learning fully implemented in selected school sites requires large sums of money from NASDC. During the 1994–95 school year, for instance, the Dubuque school district will spend approximately $250,000, mostly on staff development and resources to help teachers develop curriculum units called learning expeditions for their students.

Mountains and Valleys

School executives and teachers who prefer desk jobs might not find Expeditionary Learning appealing, especially since it's connected to Outward Bound, an organization known for putting youngsters and adults through extreme physical challenges in the outdoors. But school leaders shouldn't assume that every learning expedition has to be a wilderness adventure.

It's true that, in many cases, students go on day trips—and even overnights—as part of such programs. For instance, LaVerne Christian, an English teacher, and Paul Herdman, an Outward Bound instructor, took eighteen students from Harlem's George Washington High School rock climbing on Panther Mountain in the Catskills. (Christian and Herdman teach an experiential learning class together.)

According to Herdman, the goal was to "create a seamless curriculum" that would bring the classroom and the mountains together. Rock climbing, in this case, became a metaphor for examining all the walls youths in a dangerous inner-city neighborhood face in their daily lives.

But most learning expeditions aren't meant to be mini-adventures that involve rappelling down mountains, crossing rivers on rope bridges, foraging for food in the wilderness, or engaging in other rigorous activities often associated with Outward Bound.

Rocky Mountain School of Expeditionary Learning (Denver) student Andy Chapman scales the vertical wall of the ropes course. Photograph by David Cornwell.

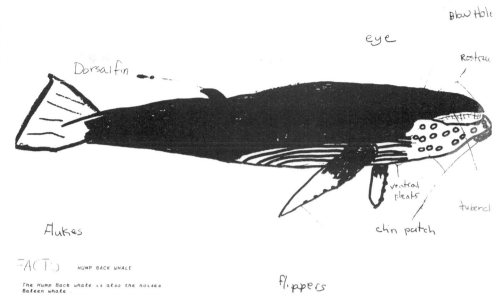

Rafael Hernandez School fourth-grade student Maynor Sanchez drew this humpback whale as part of the learning expedition "Marine Mammals: Into the Deep Blue Sea."

In fact, in most learning expeditions, students spend about three-quarters of their time studying in classrooms and about one-quarter of their time doing fieldwork. In New York's School for the Physical City, for example, an expedition titled "Our City, Ourselves" brings students only as far as library archives to search out information on immigrants. And in the King Middle School in Portland, Maine, students participating in a learning expedition called "Dream On" worked with architects at their school site to design blueprints for a new sixth-grade wing.

What matters more than where students learn, says Meg Campbell, the executive director of Expeditionary Learning Outward Bound, is whether students experience two essential ingredients—challenge and emotion—during their journeys. To intensify teaching and learning, Campbell and her associates at Expeditionary Learning maintain that teachers (or "expeditionary leaders," as they're often called) must design learning journeys with ten key principles in mind. These nonnegotiable principles, derived from the writings and practice of Kurt Hahn, the founder of Outward Bound, as well as Eleanor Duckworth and the late Paul Ylvisaker—both associated with Harvard University—provide the framework for every learning expedition in Expeditionary Learning schools.

The principles state, for instance, that teachers need to help students tap into their own potential as learners—what Campbell and others at Expeditionary Learning call "self-discovery"—and that teachers need to be sure students have time to reflect on their learning journey alone, with other students, and with adults. Another principle, drawn from Duckworth's text *The Having of Wonderful Ideas,* insists that teachers must promote opportunities for children to question, explore, and discover during their learning expeditions.

But, as teachers using Expeditionary Learning are discovering, it's one thing to have a list of guiding principles and another to make day-to-day learning go smoothly. For one thing, teachers need to find ways to meet their district's curriculum requirements. Having to satisfy two sets of guidelines—those for learning expeditions and those for district mandates—involves "some give-and-take," as one teacher puts it. For another, teachers—especially at the high school level—have to struggle with problems such as rigid schedules and graduation credits to make learning expeditions work. In many ways, teachers and school executives working to use Expeditionary Learning in their own schools and classrooms often find themselves facing their own challenges. Among Expeditionary Learning's requirements, with which they are expected to comply, are eliminating ability grouping and tracking, scheduling students and teachers to remain together for more than one year, linking community and health organizations to the schools, promoting professional development, and holding budgets in line.

As Harry Grant, a teacher in Portland, says in the journal he kept while in training at Maine's Hurricane Island Outward Bound School, "Education is a journey consisting of mountaintop experiences and valleys of doubt." To rise up and out of the valleys, Grant reminds himself and other teachers to "let

Mindie Hodgden, a student at Jack Elementary School in Portland, Maine, drills with help from teacher Ken Spinney as part of a shed building project. Photograph by David Cornwell.

learning happen" without putting barriers in the way. As Grant sees it, teachers can make or break a school's efforts to adopt Expeditionary Learning. On the one hand, they can fight efforts to adjust schedules, regroup students, and rewrite curriculum. On the other hand, they can agree to experiment with new methods and strategies to increase students' learning.

The Journey Within

At the heart of Expeditionary Learning are the principles of Outward Bound. Thomas James, professor of education at Brown University, describes Outward Bound—a program that takes its name from the nautical term for a ship heading out from port on a sea journey—as a philosophy of education that teaches students traits such as perseverance, teamwork, leadership, and compassion through challenge and adventure. In "The Only Mountain Worth Climbing," James traces the education vision of

Outward Bound's founder. As early as 1913, Hahn began to dream of an "ideal school." Hahn's ideas that learning ought to be balanced between action and reflection—he insisted that students have time each day for solitude and silence—and that students should develop moral and civic virtue through self-discovery and community service became the founding principles for the schools he designed in Germany and Scotland.

When Outward Bound formally began in 1941, Hahn envisioned having youngsters develop their will to strive for mastery by taking on physical challenges. As Tom James notes, Hahn "borrowed" beliefs from Plato—namely that individuals should strive for an "equilibrium sustained by harmony and balance" in their personal development, and that individuals can, through their personal striving, improve the society they live in. The belief in the power of "transformative experiences" to change students' behavior also shows up in school programs such as adventure-based education and experiential education, two spin-offs of Outward Bound.

Just as Outward Bound keeps the focus on how the outdoor experience affects students instead of on the experience itself, Expeditionary Learning emphasizes what students are learning over and above their journey. "It's so easy to get caught up in the excitement of a learning expedition—especially one where kids are doing exciting things like creating an art gallery or building a sailing ship," says an expeditionary guide. "We constantly need to stop and consider what the . . . experience is teaching students."

In fact, Expeditionary Learning Outward Bound requires that learning take place along four interconnected dimensions: reflection, collaboration, inquiry, and development of skills. Teachers must plan learning expeditions to include opportunities for students to contemplate (and thereby deepen and internalize) their learning; work together on teams to achieve goals; formulate questions and plan the direction of their learning; and demonstrate technical proficiency through final products and presentations. Along the way teachers also need to open up avenues so students can, in some way, contribute to their larger community—whether it be the school, neighborhood, or city.

Don Tritt, professor of psychology at Ohio's Denison University, points out that having students understand themselves as learners—what Tritt refers to as "cognitions of self"—is a necessary goal in experiential education. It's important, Tritt argues, for teachers to help students understand both their

School for the Physical City (New York) students gather in a circle to share and to discuss their experiences in the Minisink expedition. Photograph by David Cornwell.

experiences and their feelings during learning. Students, Tritt says, constantly put their self-concepts at risk—and that's especially true during Expeditionary Learning where they are encouraged to take chances. As Tritt says, students need a firm level of support from kind, considerate teachers when they "venture into uncertainty, express spontaneous ideas, or flounder and find themselves alone."

Teachers, Tritt proposes, should always turn students' learning experiences—successful or not—into reflective exercises based on two considerations. First, students should think about how they choose, judge, and evaluate ideas; second, students should think of various approaches they might use in their learning journeys. Most important, Tritt says, is that students should appreciate that what they learn about themselves is just as important as what they learn about the subjects they're investigating.

The journey inward is an important part of the Expeditionary Learning design. Drawing from the theory of experiential learning, learning should follow four steps: (1) action that gives a student concrete experience; (2) time for the student to reflect on the experience; (3) opportunity for the student to develop concepts and generalizations; and (4) chances to apply reflection and learning to a new experience.

A job teachers can't overlook, Tritt says, is providing students with a repertoire of words to describe their learning experiences, as well as opportunities to articulate their thoughts and emotions. By providing these, teachers can keep students from getting lost during their learning journeys.

Teachers at the Core

Will Expeditionary Learning designs take hold in traditional schools? Can new schools be founded on its theory and principles? Yes, Expeditionary Learning officials say, if teachers are treated as key to the process. That's why teachers in Expeditionary Learning's experimental sites are immersed in professional development that involves summer summits, minisabbaticals, and one-day explorations. In fact, the whole notion of Expeditionary Learning for students depends on getting their teachers to become learners too.

Week-long summits held in the summer of 1994, for instance, had teachers get involved in learning expeditions centered on architecture, geology, and the Cherokee Nation. Becoming students and "learning to learn" are the objectives of each summit, says Leah Rugen, associate director of Expeditionary Learning. But, according to Rugen, taking part in the expeditions also prompts teachers to examine their classroom practice and consider the changes they'll need to make as they adopt the expeditionary approach in their home schools. Two concepts prevail during summits and other staff development programs, Rugen states: teacher-as-learner and teacher-as-constructor of knowledge. (In other words, teachers need to learn how to learn right along with their students, and teachers need to develop ideas and strategies as they conduct learning experiences with their classes.)

The concept that drives professional development, say Expeditionary Learning leaders, is having teachers undergo an "inner transformation" before expecting them to change their teaching. Putting teachers through learning expeditions and helping them understand their experiences are both ways of changing the culture of a school. As Michael Fullan, a teacher development expert, notes, teachers need to take an inquiring approach if there's to be change in school practice; they also need to collaborate among themselves and with their administrators, refine and develop new technical skills, and take time to reflect on what they're learning and teaching.

Teachers with spirit—those who already bring challenge and emotion to their classrooms—are lining up with the advocates of Expeditionary Learning. But given the need to reform many school practices (such as tracking and scheduling)—and

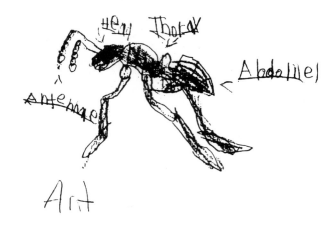

Kindergarten-student Israel F. Roloh, of the Rafael Hernandez School in Boston, sketched this ant during a learning expedition on insects.

given the large-scale commitment schools need to make to professional development—it's not quite as certain that large numbers of public schools will join in the journey. ◆

Susan Black is an education consultant in Hammondsport, New York.

Part Five

Recasting Professional Development

Through this kind of teaching, I feel I am really able to practice my craft. I am valued as a professional and I am never stifled. Each expedition offers me an opportunity to learn. That is an important quality for my students to see.

—Teacher
Academy for Educational Development Evaluation

From the Inside Out:

The Expeditionary Learning Process of Teacher Change

Denis Udall and Leah Rugen

Teachers as Learners

In a rural North Carolina town a group of teachers is putting the final touches on its closing arguments. The "attorneys" representing the United States government huddle in one corner, those for the Cherokee Nation in another. The issue: Is the removal of the Cherokee to the west, the infamous Trail of Tears, inevitable, or is there a way out? In

Teachers as learners. It is a simple idea. But teacher educators are increasingly appreciating its appeal and power for shaping the professional lives of educators.

the adjacent room, a panel of White and Cherokee "judges" await the oral arguments. The teachers are keenly aware that this issue is not the dry, remote past, but a living history in which the Cherokee people are still invested; they deeply care about how history will judge them and their ancestors.

Teachers as learners. It is a simple idea. But teacher educators are increasingly appreciating its appeal and power for shaping the professional lives of educators.

Expeditionary Learning Outward Bound's approach to teacher development begins with a simple proposition: when teachers view themselves as learners, they enhance their capacity to reflect on their craft in ways that help them do it better. Our experience has taught us that when teachers have lived an educational experience and reflected on their own growth as learners, they are better able to grasp its educational value and later reap its rewards in their classrooms.

Summits immerse teachers in weeklong "learning expeditions" focused on a particular subject.

When teachers seek to improve their instruction and build relationships with others in their profession, the most common option available to them is to enroll in a workshop or course. Few of these, however, are truly energizing. They perpetuate ineffective modes of teaching: teachers are taught at, they are instructed in strategies or in the use of materials that have been researched by scholars, encapsulated by curriculum experts, and disseminated by staff developers. At some point, teachers are evaluated on how well they implement the "innovations." In short, they are seen as consumers of information and techniques, lacking in skill and in need of training rather than thoughtful professionals who have a capacity to reflect on their craft in ways that might allow them to improve.

Over the past two years we have been experimenting with a professional development experience—called a summit—that draws on teachers' knowledge about their craft while introducing them to new practices and subject matter. Summits immerse teachers in week-long "learning expeditions" focused on a particular subject. During the week, participants observe and work with a master teacher. Throughout, they are confronted with complex problems and practices that invite searching questions and making deep connections. The content must be

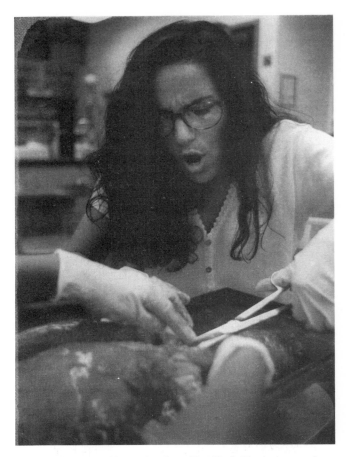

Abbe Kirsch, a health teacher from New York City, reacts to the task of dissecting a pig's heart and lungs during the summit Bodies in Tune. Photograph by Mark Hirsch for the Telegraph Herald.

sophisticated, and the tasks must be compelling and challenging, but within reach.

Summits model the active, adventurous learning that Expeditionary Learning teachers and schools are striving to engage in with their students. A teacher who participates may return home with the framework and content for a specific interdisciplinary unit. Another teacher may take away a set of teaching practices that cut across subject matter and topic. Most important, summits create the opportunity for all teachers to reflect on themselves as learners, to deepen their inquiry about their practice, and to think about ways to integrate what they learn into their own classrooms.

As simple a notion as teachers as learners is, we have found it complex to translate into practice. What kinds of learning experiences are most valuable to teachers? What is the right balance of immersion into learning and reflection on teaching? What support is necessary to help teachers transfer their experience as learners into classroom practice? Questions like these have come up again and again in our shaping summits as vehicles for teacher development.

Following is a journal by Leah Rugen written while attending an Expeditionary Learning summit about the Cherokee Nation Trail of Tears. The summit, taught by Bill Anderson (a professor of history at Western Carolina University) and Leo Snow (a middle school teacher at The Children's School in Morganton, North Carolina), was held in Cullowhee, North Carolina. Other Expeditionary Learning summits have included Architecture (led by Ron Berger and Russann Cook), and Geology (led by Ron Berger and John Reid). In the section immediately following the journal we will explore the above questions, as well as discuss several important aspects of summits related to the professional development of teachers.

The Treaty of New Echota— Living Painful Ambiguity

Cullowhee, North Carolina

Monday evening: As we drive west from Asheville to the site of the summit, Leo Snow tells us that we are entering a land that Cherokee in Oklahoma still claim as their own. It will be powerful to be in a place so laden with history and to have a chance to study it deeply.

The questions and our task are compelling and scary. What brought about the "fraudulent Treaty of New Echota," which forced the Trail of Tears to occur? Was it inevitable? We are to take on the character of one of a number of historical figures and thoroughly research him (I assume there are no women—hmmmm?). Can we imagine our character renegotiating a better treaty—given the historical context and our character's makeup? The questions are daunting by themselves, but adding to the challenge, we are going to present a new version of the treaty to an actual judge, and possibly to a panel of Cherokee. I have to admit I am wondering at this moment if it's possible to do all this in five short days.

Day two: After Leo and Bill Anderson give us an overview of the culture, history, and economics of the nineteenth-century Cherokee, we each draw the name of the character we will research and role-play. The drawing generates a great deal of suspense. We have no control over our choices, and there is a lot of apprehension about drawing the name of a "villain." The teacher who has been secretly wishing "please don't let me pick Andrew Jackson" indeed draws his name.

We spend the afternoon in the library following leads provided by Bill and Leo, or digging on our own. It's strange to sit in a modern, air-conditioned library and read the letters of John Grey Bynum, a twenty-five-year-old lieutenant who went to Cherokee territory hoping to establish his military career. I get chills as I realize that in only a few weeks he is transformed from an officer determined to carry out his duty with cool detachment—"I am persuaded that with the force here I can clear the valley in one week"—to a man who deeply questions his orders and begins to feel sympathetic toward the Cherokee—"I am very much interested in favor of this family . . . The old members of the family are too old to remove."

Day three: I've reached a low point. The initial excitement has worn off, and I am not sure of where

the whole process is going. Tired of reading and research, I long for the liveliness of the group's discussions, and our probing and debating the ideas and issues that surround our different characters. I push through until lunchtime, when we pile into vans and head to the Cherokee reservation. This experience becomes the week's turning point for me.

◆ ◆ ◆

The questions are daunting by themselves, but adding to the challenge, we are going to present a new version of the treaty to an actual judge, and possibly to a panel of Cherokee.

◆ ◆ ◆

As a community service project, we clean out a densely overgrown cemetery. Bill is eager to see if we can find the grave of Yonaguska, one of the Cherokee leaders at the time of the Trail of Tears. I begin to lose my feeling of isolation in the camaraderie that comes with this physical task. Together we slash through weeds and bushes, trying to avoid the copious poison ivy. We finish clearing a steep path, and arrive at the entrance to the cemetery. In a couple of hours we clear a space around the gravesites, where, to our delight, we locate a rock pile that is probably Yonaguska's grave. It seems that by honoring the dead we have honored the past and present—and have engaged with this subject physically as well as intellectually.

That evening we return to the town of Cherokee for a traditional Cherokee dinner. We are joined by ten members of the Crowe, Wolfe, and Junaluska families, who span three generations. After getting acquainted over dinner, Leo asks an opening question. The evening passes in a fascinating rush of remembrances and ideas. The families speak of contemporary tribal politics, child-rearing practices, and the importance of their large, extended families. They share their commitment to the well-being of

A teacher digs for crystals at the Geology Summit: Rocks, Rivers and Caves. Photograph by Elizabeth Maynard.

the Cherokee Nation, and some speak with eloquent passion about past injustices. For almost two hours they share their lives with generosity and kindness. Sitting in a circle in the twilight, listening intently to the talk, I not only feel more connected to my fellow students but also imagine that at least briefly we have formed a wider community.

Day four: Suddenly there is only a day left to prepare for presenting our characters. We don't possibly have enough time. We spend half the day reading, writing notes, and thinking about how we will make our character come alive. We each have five minutes to make a presentation, and we're counting on using what we learn to carry out the negotiation of a new treaty. The teachers express the same kinds of anxiety that we have all heard from our students: "I haven't read enough," "I hate public speaking," "I hope people don't confuse me with my character." There is even a sprinkling of competition as we note who has been studying into the wee hours.

Day five: For over two and a half hours I sit riveted, taking notes, as people bring their characters to life. Some have composed speeches that they deliver with passionate oratory. Some enlist others for an improvised role-play. Everyone speaks in the first person and, though there is a lot of laughter, we approach our characters with deep seriousness. The presentations are a wonderful vehicle for us to teach each other about the complex and intercon-

necting forces of the time: racism, the different factions within the Cherokee Nation, the pressure of states' rights and the threat of secession, competing concepts of military duty and honor, those clergy who supported versus those who opposed the removal, and the extreme economic pressure of land speculation and the massive westward immigration. It's exhilarating but overwhelming. How will we

◆ ◆ ◆

It seems that by honoring the dead we have honored the past and present—and have engaged with this subject physically as well as intellectually.

◆ ◆ ◆

ever negotiate a new treaty? Do we have to accept the removal of the Cherokee as inevitable, or is there a way out?

With the knowledge that we'll present our treaty to a panel of White and Cherokee judges, we plunge into negotiations. Initially we break into two large groups. One group is predominantly Cherokee and

Teachers clear a Cherokee cemetery as a service project for the Treaty of New Echota Summit. Photograph by Leah Rugen.

is emphatically opposed to removal. The other represents "government interests," though its members are joined by the faction of Cherokee who had signed the original Treaty of New Echota and supported the move west. The negotiation extends into the evening. Teachers in leadership roles play them to the hilt, while others provide council, ask questions, and play devil's advocate. The role-plays are tested through this process. Some find it extremely difficult to stay in character. Their personal views and emotions keep entering the debate. Others interpret their roles strictly. It's difficult for everyone, but especially for those who must take on roles of people with views antithetical to their own.

Initially, each group develops a separate treaty. But after proposing them to the other side, we have to go back to the drawing board and contend with the other side's nonnegotiables. When we are on the verge of reaching one unified "compromise treaty," Leo stirs things up again by prompting people to hold on to their deeply held convictions, and to resist the urge to reach an easy compromise so we can all get to bed. When we finally do call it a night we have two treaties, both of which acknowledge the inevitability of dislocation. One treaty represents a united Cherokee position. It ensures much greater financial security than the government's version and insists on full sovereignty for the Cherokee Nation. Everyone feels that we are going into the next day's defense with less than complete understanding and a lot of questions.

The exercise of trying to unite competing points of view while respecting historical reality raises many painful questions. Is our compromise a pragmatic, necessary choice, or a selling out of principle? If the extermination of the Cherokee people was inevitable, if they had resisted moving west, should we support removal? Can history be reimagined in a way that takes account of what we have learned from tragic outcomes, but also fully acknowledges the complex, actual forces of the time?

Day six: We enter the "formal hearing" to present and defend our treaties with a high degree of anxiety knowing that representatives of the Cherokee people and a federal judge will be our audience. The two treaties are reviewed and intensely questioned and scrutinized. Each character is called to the stand and asked to give an opinion. Leo and Bill act as "friends of the court" offering their own questions and making certain the judges do not leave out any vital issues. When the judges finally offer their sum-

mary analysis of what they have heard, it is a bit anticlimactic, since by now we know that there is no satisfying resolution, only painful ambiguity.

When we assemble for a final circle to debrief the week, we take a moment and release the spirits of the past and just be ourselves. It will take time to make sense of all we've learned, but in the hour-long discussion people speak of how important it was to be a student again and of the support they got from the group. There will be ample opportunity to apply what we've learned to designing learning expeditions for our classrooms. But for now we appreciate that by focusing on a single historical character, we have opened up the world of the nineteenth-century Cherokee.

Themes and Lessons

Having experienced summits as learners ourselves, we have closely examined their commonalities. Beyond their basic structure—the compelling topic, the projects, the expectations for performance—there are dimensions that make summits powerful learning experiences that we can see more clearly in hindsight. We are also faced with new questions that present opportunities to redesign and improve future summits.

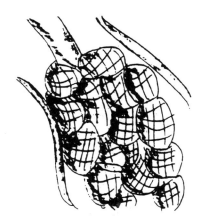

Michelle A. Mejia, a teacher at the Rafael Hernandez School in Boston, drew this illustration of the alveoli, air sacs in the lung, for the physiology summit, Bodies in Tune.

Real-World Contexts for Learning

Summits are a break from professional development as usual. Content is not presented in a linear progression from basic to more complex understandings. Nor are teachers taught a set of specific skills or methodologies. Rather, they are faced with complex, real-life conundrums and dilemmas—their own and those of others. Forced to pick their own way through sticky problems and questions, they make mistakes, get help from others, note where their understanding leaves off, and note what they do about what they do not know. In short, they "accept surprise, puzzlement, excitement, patience, caution, honest attempts, and wrong outcomes as legitimate and important elements of learning."[1]

Lisa Schneier writes, "We sand away at the interesting edges of subject matter until it is so free from its natural complexities, so neat, that there is not a crevice left as an opening. All that is left is to

◆ ◆ ◆

It will take time to make sense of all we've learned, but in the hour-long discussion people speak of how important it was to be a student again.

◆ ◆ ◆

hand it to them [learners], scrubbed and smooth, so they can view it as outsiders."[2] Summits attempt to respect and present subject matter in all its complexity, and in doing so "make it more accessible by opening a multiplicity of paths into it."[3]

Summits also present teachers with the rare opportunity to learn together and participate in a community of teacher-learners. Summits offer teachers an experience of a group as greater than the sum of its parts. Each person makes a unique contribution to everyone's learning. Explicit attention to building this community of learners and shaping rich and meaningful content creates context and purpose for learning.

Generative Topics

Summits have taught us about choosing subject matter that lends itself to "teaching for understanding."[4] Not all topics are created equal. Some "invite understanding performances of diverse kinds" that more readily connect to learners' unfolding ideas and beliefs and are better able to extend learners'

thinking. "Many topics taught in the conventional treatment of the subject matter do not appear to be very generative. They are not chosen for their outreach, their import, their connectibility."[5]

David Perkins suggests that topics that are at the heart of a pedagogy of understanding have:

Centrality—topics should be central to subject matter or a domain of knowledge
Accessibility—topics should allow and invite performance of teachers' and students' understandings rather than being spare or arcane
Richness—topics should encourage making connections to diverse subjects inside and outside the discipline, and building on learners' prior knowledge

Based on our experience, we would add that topics should also engage learners' emotions and passions for learning.

The Treaty of New Echota summit is generative in the sense that participants began with only a vague understanding of the historical importance of the treaty and the Trail of Tears. Through the course of their investigation into the lives of their characters, their questions generated new ones. The leaders of the summit did not know in advance the outcome of the treaty-making process or the trial. There were parameters, but no prescribed solutions or answers. Because the topic touched on powerful themes of racism, morality, economic forces, and individual choice, the study generated a great deal of emotion and personal soul-searching.

Innovation from the Inside

Typically, staff developers seek to bring about change in the beliefs, views, and perceptions of teachers. Historically, for instance, these efforts have been aimed at convincing teachers of the efficacy of a certain instructional practice or in changing their beliefs about how a particular subject matter should be taught. Most teacher development models are based on the idea that it is critical to get teacher commitment and acceptance of an innovation before a training takes place. The underlying assumption is that changing teachers' ideas, beliefs, or perceptions results in specific changes in teachers' classroom practices, which in turn leads to improvement in student outcomes.[6] But researchers have found "that significant change in the beliefs and attitudes of teachers is contingent in their gaining evidence of change in learning outcomes of their students." In other words, completely adopting a practice or innovation is likely to occur only after a teacher sees evidence of students' learning.[7] This turns the traditional teacher development model on its head: change in teachers' classroom practices, and ultimately their beliefs and attitudes, comes through seeing firsthand the effects the proposed change has on student learning.

◆ ◆ ◆

This turns the traditional teacher development model on its head: change in teachers' classroom practices, and ultimately their beliefs and attitudes, comes through seeing firsthand the effects the proposed change has on student learning.

◆ ◆ ◆

We think that this is an important insight into how teachers come to change their practice, but that it misses a key point we have discovered in the course of our work. Not only do teachers need to see growth in students' learning to believe in the efficacy of an innovation, but their beliefs and attitudes about teaching are deeply affected when they experience and reflect upon their own growth—that is, when they come to understand the impact of an innovation through their own lived experience. In turn, teachers lend a critical degree of meaning and viability to an innovation through their efforts to make sense of it.

Bridging into Practice

This brings us to perhaps the thorniest question we have been faced with in designing summits: What does all this mean for how teachers practice their craft back in their classrooms? Professional development facilitators typically assume that transfer

takes care of itself. In fact, if summits were modeled after a traditional staff development workshop, we would assume that whatever practices were imparted to teachers would be adopted without a great deal of alteration. But as we have seen, summits are rooted in a wholly different approach. Not only are teachers expected not to implement mechanistically a summit in their classroom, but many attended summits that had little if anything to do with the subject matter they teach in school. Thus we have been forced to ask ourselves, "How can cognitive skills and teaching practices that teachers gain in one context be useful to them in another context that might have very little in common with where these skills and practices were originally acquired?"

At issue here is a question that has long fascinated cognitive psychologists: Are the kinds of thoughtful performances that we find in summits generalizable to other contexts, or are they relatively

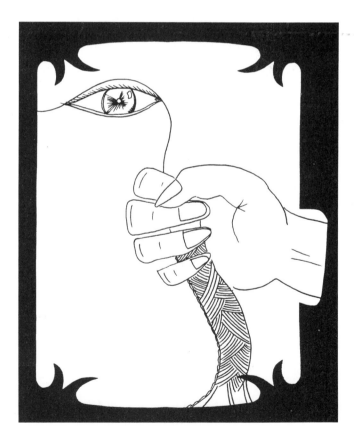

At an annual principals' conference, David Olson, principal of Central Alternative High School in Dubuque, Iowa, depicted two design principles that illustrate his vision of education. His image of the hand grabbing the rope represents The Responsibility for Learning, and the eye symbolizes Service and Compassion.

Molly Melville and Amanda Kessler of the Rafael Hernandez School in Boston are captivated by the storybook that they are reading together. Photograph by David Cornwell.

context bound? Much of the research on transfer suggests that "thinking at its most effective depends on specific, context-bound skills and units of knowledge that have little application to other domains. To the extent that transfer does take place, it is highly specific and must be cued, primed and guided; it seldom occurs spontaneously."[8] This is sometimes called the problem of "local knowledge." Skills and knowledge are more local and specific than general or transferable.[9] It might seem that this observation would not bode well for professional development designs such as summits. A summit, after all, is designed to help teachers appreciate how they grapple with unfamiliar terrain and how their minds and those of others take hold of subject matter, in the context of learning specific skills. These understandings are not exactly made for easy transfer. In fact, one could argue that due to their relative abstractness these skills are difficult to transport to different settings.

Our experience has taught us that transfer is possible, but that it requires that we mediate the process of teachers' abstracting lessons from one setting and making connections to others. As might be expected, the key is connecting what teachers learn during summits to their prior knowledge. Summits are designed for this kind of cognitive "bridging," or the "deliberate mindful abstraction of a skill or knowledge from one context for application in another."[10] Indeed, we have learned that there is a continuum along which most summit participants fall—from faithfully replicating a summit in its entirety to reflecting on its abstract, but no less powerful, lessons for practice. One writing teacher found that a geology summit helped her to think better about how to work in an interdisciplinary team.

The summit gave me a place to feel comfortable within a science classroom. I know a lot about history so I've always felt comfortable collaborating with social studies teachers, but I've stayed away from the sciences because I was less familiar with them. But

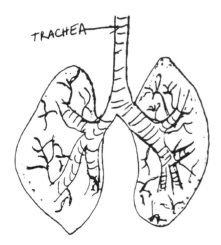

Michelle A. Mejia, a teacher at the Rafael Hernandez School in Boston, drew this illustration of the trachea and lungs for the physiology summit, Bodies in Tune.

now I'm more able to see my place in a science class and see ways I can connect it to writing. The way interdisciplinary work usually happens is that students come to me and say, "Will you help me write this science paper?" That interests me less than doing the science along with them and helping them to develop a thesis. I'd rather have insight in what they're doing because I've been through it with them.

Another teacher welcomed the opportunity to focus on teaching:

One reason the summit worked well for me is that I was out of my own domain. The fact that I had to step outside of my content area gave me a whole new set of insights into teaching. It forced me to look at the learning and not just the content. When I take professional development workshops within my domain I often get caught up in what is being taught rather than how it's being taught. The summit taught me that there was something important about removing myself from my comfort zone that allowed me to see teaching from a different angle.

Summits allow each teacher to walk away with his or her own ideas for improving practice. For some, a faithful replication of a summit helps them to gain insight into how to design an interdisciplinary, thematic, project-based expedition. For others, for whom the subject matter may not be relevant, a summit can be an opportunity to experience the process of expeditionary learning and to reflect on their practice. We have learned that for either to occur we need to build in opportunities for teachers to bridge into practice by "reaching forward"—that is, taking stock of what they learn in anticipation of applying it in new and different contexts, and "reaching backward" into their past experience to make connections with problems and questions they have confronted during summits.[11]

Social Dimensions of Learning

Summits are expeditions into the unknown. In the same way that an expedition to a remote mountain range requires its members to prepare carefully and to pool their efforts, so too a summit is designed to encourage teachers to collaborate intensely with one another on a shared outcome in which they are all deeply invested. Teachers are encouraged to build a community of learning where they work toward common goals and work products that could only be accomplished by drawing upon the talents, passions, and efforts of the entire group. Indeed the founder of Outward Bound, Kurt Hahn, keenly understood the educative power of small groups. He believed that in intimate settings leadership abilities can emerge that are present but inhibited in most people. Moreover, Hahn believed that through shared commitment a genuine community begins to take shape. He saw that one of the key aims of schools was to "harmonize the social and intellectual differences between students by operating as a community of participation and active service" where students mediate their own personal goals within the context of a larger moral purpose.[12] Moral purpose emerges both from the commitment and structure of community and from the nature of the questions and problems studied.

The Cherokee Nation "Trail of Tears" summit challenged participants' values and emotions as well as their ability to reason. It created a learning environment in which everyone's efforts were needed to advance the understanding of all. The group was faced with the seemingly impossible task of understanding a complex period of history and preparing a sophisticated performance of this understanding in five days. Through the intersection of intellectual challenge and community, real learning occurred.

Our future challenge will be to design more opportunities during summits for teachers to make thoughtful abstractions and then to discover meaningful connections with their classrooms and school communities. ◆

1. Eleanor Duckworth, *"The Having of Wonderful Ideas" and Other Essays on Teaching and Learning.* (New York: Teacher's College Press, 1987), p. 69.
2. Lisa Schneier, "Why Not Just Say It?" (unpublished manuscript, Harvard Graduate School of Education, May 1990), p. 1.
3. Duckworth.
4. Howard Gardner and Veronica Boix-Mansilla, "Teaching for Understanding—Within and Across the Disciplines," Educational Leadership 51:5 (1994), pp. 14–18.
5. David Perkins, *Smart Schools: From Training Memories to Educating Minds* (New York: Free Press, 1992), pp. 92–93.
6. Thomas Guskey, "Staff Development and the Process of Teacher Change," Educational Researcher (May 1986), pp. 5–12.
7. Ibid, p. 7.

8. David Perkins, "Are Cognitive Skills Context-Bound?" *Educational Researcher* (Jan.–Feb. 1989), p. 19.

9. David Perkins, "Teaching for Transfer," *Educational Leadership* (Sept. 1988), p. 24.

10. Ibid, p. 25.

11. Ibid, p. 26.

12. Thomas James, "The Only Mountain Worth Climbing: An Historical and Philosophical Exploration of Outward Bound and Its Link to Education," in *Fieldwork: An Expeditionary Learning Outward Bound Reader* (Dubuque, Iowa: Kendall/Hunt, 1995), p. 66.

Leah Rugen is the associate director of Expeditionary Learning Outward Bound. Denis Udall is a school designer with Expeditionary Learning Outward Bound.

From Summit to Learning Expeditions—Teachers to Students

Amy Mednick

C learing out an overgrown cemetery on the Cherokee reservation in Cherokee, North Carolina, last summer, fifth-grade teacher Beverly Graves suddenly felt as though she were searching for her own burial site.

The Bryant Elementary School (Dubuque, Iowa) teacher Graves was participating with twenty other educators in Expeditionary Learning Outward Bound's Treaty of New Echota Summit, a week-long professional development learning expedition focusing on the Cherokee Nation's forced removal from the South. At the summit, each participant assumed the role of a historic figure, delving into the character's personal history and reflecting on his or her words, beliefs, and actions.

Fifth-grade teacher Graves played Cherokee leader Chief Yonaguska. Beneath the weeds and underbrush at the cemetery, the group was searching for Yonaguska's grave.

Experiencing that powerful interaction with a character in history convinced Graves and team teacher Barbara Egan, who also attended the summit, that producing a play on the Cherokee Nation's forced removal from the South would transform just another chapter in a history text into a personal and meaningful learning expedition for the children, Graves said.

Transported from the hills of North Carolina to a school auditorium in Dubuque six months later, Graves and Egan brought home the lessons learned and produced the play *Cherokee Removal*.

William Anderson, a history professor at Western Carolina University in Cullowhee, was a coleader of the Cherokee summit with Leo Snow, a teacher at the Children's School in Morganton, North Carolina. Anderson said he expected teachers to gain knowledge of the historical events and an empathy for the history of the Cherokee people.

"I've done workshops before, but very seldom is there follow-up. The teachers in Dubuque almost became fanatical about it, and I mean that in the good sense," Anderson said. "They kept saying I inspired them, but I've never seen someone so inspired before."

Transported from the hills of North Carolina to a school auditorium in Dubuque six months later, Graves and Egan brought home the lessons learned and produced the play *Cherokee Removal.*

Graves and Egan expanded on an existing play with help from Anderson. By the time *Cherokee Removal* was performed in January, the students were immersed in Native American history and culture.

Artwork by fifth grader Andy Ironside, of Bryant Elementary School in Dubuque, Iowa, illustrates the program of the play Cherokee Removal.

"It was so exciting to see kids in the hall saying, 'Hey, I'm going to try out for John Martin, the Cherokee Supreme Court Justice.' This was everybody, not just talented and gifted kids," Graves said.

"I think sometimes these experiences just become part of you and the way you express things to children or explain your enthusiasm, it becomes part of your personality and the children see that," said Egan, who teaches fourth grade.

After he spoke to students in Dubuque, Anderson said that they bombarded him with questions, which revealed their keen interest in Native Americans. "I've gotten maybe a hundred letters from the kids so far, and they were telling me some of the things they've learned and how they feel sorry for the Indians," Anderson said.

Six states away at the Rafael Hernandez School in Boston, fifth-grade teachers Eloise Biscoe and Wanda Muriel also recently finished a fall Native American learning expedition. While Biscoe did not focus the expedition specifically on the history of the Cherokee Nation, the summit inspired her approach and her goals for the class. Above all, Biscoe said, she wanted the students to understand the complexity of the issue and the perspective of each side. Biscoe said she tried to depart from the modern stereotype of vilifying the settlers and assuming every Native American to be a hero without underestimating the grand tragedy of the Native American people.

"If you get involved in one event, you begin to understand it wasn't just 'good guy, bad guy.' I wanted to show the students—without trying to detract

from the fact that in the end the Native Americans ended up with the short end of the stick—to break it down and say how it took place," she said.

Egan, at Bryant, agreed. She assumed the role of General Winfield Scott, who commanded the army's removal of the Cherokee. This allowed her to see both sides of the story. "When my students talk to me about how bad it was, I also have to give them the other side too. So, it was good for me to play that particular role," Egan said.

At Hernandez, Biscoe said she strove to improve last year's learning expedition on the encounters between Native Americans and European settlers. "The way we had done it previously, the students hadn't gotten much out of it, and they hadn't understood the complexity of the issues," Biscoe said.

A powerful work of historical fiction, *No Resting Place*, by William Humphrey, about the Cherokee Nation—reading assigned in advance of the summit—captivated Biscoe. A historically accurate novel, rather than a broad collection of nonfiction accounts, therefore would also engage the students, she said. "I felt this was an exciting way to get straight into an event," she said.

After reading the novel *Thunder Rolling in the Mountains*, by Scott O'Dell and Elizabeth Hall, Biscoe's class split into groups and wrote their own play based on the book. Each group wrote a scene, often taking direct historical quotes from the various characters. The groups then auditioned for parts, practiced the play, and pieced it together. Before this, each group had researched a tribe and put together creative

Dubuque teachers Marylou Althoff and Becky Lorenzen work on planning a learning expedition. Photograph by David Guralnick.

As if looking in a mirror, Kelly Pins and Pamela Enderson wipe their makeup off after the performance of the play Cherokee Removal, *at Bryant Elementary School in Dubuque, Iowa. Photograph by Patti Carr for the* Telegraph Herald.

dioramas covering housing, customs, and religion, and debunking some of the traditional stereotypes.

Cherokee Removal in Dubuque involved two casts of thirty-five, set designers, and costume and makeup artists for two separate productions. Teachers Lee Skaife and Ray Roberts coproduced the play. While the school had staged ten large productions before, this was the first attempt to portray a historical event.

"The children were captivated by the research because each child had a role in the play," Egan said.

In fact, one parent wrote a letter to Graves, which included a short anecdote about her daughter. After the performance, the girl told her mother that she had to talk to Anderson. He was chatting with the district superintendent, but the mother let her daughter go over. She waited her turn and then asked Anderson if her character, Chief Agili, had died on the Trail of Tears.

"She just had to know. That's how much she was into her character. That incident spoke volumes to me," the mother said.

Graves said the play production really exemplified Expeditionary Learning's principles, and that the cast became a family during the production. "The collaboration was just five stars," Graves said. "They found out that it doesn't make any difference if you're a set designer, on lights, sound, the star, or have one line, it doesn't work unless everyone pulls together and collaborates." ◆

Amy Mednick is the editor of The Web.

In a learning expedition on Native Americans inspired by the Cherokee summit, fifth-grade children at the Rafael Hernandez School in Boston explain what the story of the Nez Perce means to their own lives:

◆ To me it means that to stop war we need to stop arguing and start cooperating.

◆ This story reminds me of the struggle of African Americans for equal rights and nonsegregation.

◆ The story shows me that it is important not just to look at one point of view when trying to solve a problem, but to look at other people's feelings too. Then maybe a compromise could be reached.

◆ It tells me that we are going to have to share sometime in life.

◆ The story leaves me with a question, 'Are there other ways to solve a problem besides war?'

◆ The story makes me think that violence is not the only way to solve problems.

◆ It tells me that some people have different ways of doing things and you should stand up for your rights.

Stream Day One

Ron Berger

Deep in the woods, hidden from the sun and summer heat, a team of teachers wades through a shaded stream, clipboards and tools in hand. Armed with measuring tape, string, nails, protractors, meter sticks, and surveying equipment, they shout out directions, distances, angles; they argue over figures, test new techniques, flail at insects, laugh, lose their balance.

Spectators gather on the mossy bank above them: visitors from the Cambridge Expeditionary Learning Outward Bound office, a film crew from New York City, preparing a video on New American Schools' designs, even a farmer with a bushy beard who heard a commotion in the woods and left his tractor in the field. But the audience does not distract these intrepid researchers. They are excited, confused, intent on their work. A serious group of budding scientists.

I lean against a wide treetrunk and watch the commotion below. I am the only one aware that most of the measurements being taken are invalid, most of the data is unusable. And moreover, the mistakes being made in data collection and group organization will be the seeds for great learning, far more important than the data itself. Still, it is hard

> I lean against a wide treetrunk and watch the commotion below. I am the only one aware that most of the measurements being taken are invalid, most of the data is unusable.

to watch the confusion and experimenting inherent in beginning investigations and not intervene with teacherly advice: "Do it this way . . . Start here . . . That won't work . . . Set yourselves up at regular intervals." But I hold back.

This was day five of the Geology Summit: Rocks, Rivers, and Caves, held in Amherst, Massachusetts. We had slithered through caves together, climbed mountains, investigated rocks, and were in our final phase—rivers and streams. After eight months of planning, the summit was unfolding beautifully: great teamwork, excitement, adventure, learning. It was not unfolding precisely as planned, because

Teachers, along with a parent, dam a stream bed during the Geology Summit: Rocks Rivers and Caves. Photograph by Trina Abbott.

what expedition really does, or should? Each day the schedule was renegotiated with the whole group as our needs and passions evolved.

In planning this second Geology Summit, Mary Johnston, Expeditionary Learning Outward Bound's summit director, and I appraised the strengths and weaknesses of the first, last summer, and made changes. A key change was adding a second day of stream work: one day to make mistakes and get our bearings and a second day, a second draft, to redo our work as an experienced team.

The evening of our first stream research day, when the degree of mistakes became evident, teachers were discouraged, even upset. The group stared at Trina Abbott and me—their supposed leaders— as if to say, "How could you let us waste our whole

day like this!?" Our measurements had not been standardized properly, our teams overlapped and did not communicate, the tools had not been used properly. Common systems and reference points needed to be set, common practices—the best of those that emerged from Stream Day One—needed to be adopted by all. We needed to get organized.

Yet the day was anything but a waste. Stream Day Two was a whole new world. The very team members who saw little need for standardization on Day One had turned into measurement standard fanatics. We checked and rechecked, discussed and organized; time intervals were even announced with a whistle! A military drill team would have admired us. Keep in mind that none of this organization came from me. On the contrary, I was criticized at one

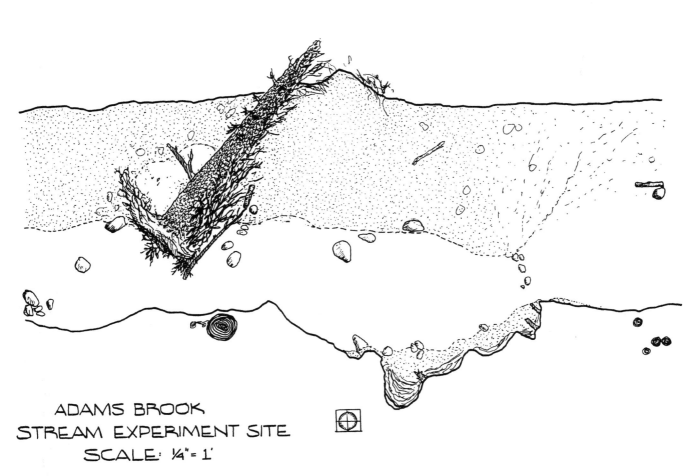

ADAMS BROOK
STREAM EXPERIMENT SITE
SCALE: ¼" = 1'

Summit leader Ron Berger sketched to scale the section of Adams Brook measured by the teachers at the geology summit Rocks, Rivers, and Caves, in Amherst, Massachusetts.

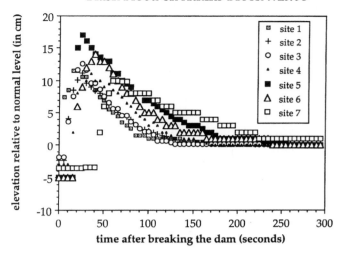

Flash Flood on Atkins Brook 7/29/95

At the Geology Summit, teachers built a dam and created a flash flood and then returned to the classroom and generated computer graphs of the work.

point for calling out time intervals too irregularly. The team, the group, forged our precision.

Stream Day Two went beyond measuring and into more complex investigations. In an experiment designed by my coleader, geologist John Reid, we built a small dam and stopped the stream flow. We positioned ourselves at regular (very regular) intervals downstream, took measurements of the streambed, and waited. When the dam could hold no more, it was torn loose, and the surging crests of the flash flood were measured by brave souls in the streambed at five-second intervals (hence the whistle and shouting). We also mapped the trajectory of numbered pebbles, laid in a straight line across the dry streambed and then tumbled by the flood.

Back in the classroom, this data was entered into a computer database, graphed, and analyzed in heated discussions. Computer-generated graphs that one day earlier would have seemed dull and lifeless, or even intimidating and indecipherable to these teachers, were now as gripping as a mystery novel. The fieldwork had built a platform of understanding that made the academics—the graphs and concepts—both accessible and exciting.

John Reid presented the data from last year's flash flood at a professional conference. This year's data set was much more accurate, and John was so impressed he announced that he would like to use it as the basis for a professional paper. Suddenly that wasted day did not seem so wasted after all. ◆

Ron Berger teaches sixth grade at Shutesbury Elementary School in Shutesbury, Massachusetts, and served as course director for the Geology Summit: Rocks, Rivers, and Caves.

Understanding Through Art

Steven Levy

I recently participated in a workshop for teachers where we explored the ten design principles of Expeditionary Learning Outward Bound. Equipped with construction paper, scissors, crayons, glue, and tape, our group was instructed to create a piece of art that represented the principle of *Solitude and Reflection*.

We began by sharing individual thoughts, listening for an organizing principle that they had in common. We visualized solitude and reflection from many points of view, pushing and challenging each other's perspectives as we strove to create an image together. What was the form of solitude? What shape was it? What color? What led to it? What followed from it? How could we represent it with the materials we had?

The discussions that the artistic challenge inspired were fascinating. Sometimes our thoughts were aligned. Other times they were opposed. Our ideas were not judged right or wrong, but rather scrutinized according to the common understanding that was emerging out of our collective experience. When the rationale for a form or color was consistent with our experience, everyone shouted, "Yeah, that's it!" If it was not, we explored what was different or incomplete, and thus further sharpened our collective understanding. In other words, we learned as much from the images we discarded as from the ones we chose.

For example, one of the teachers said, "I think it should be blue."

"Why blue?" we asked.

"Because blue is cool and reflective, unlike red, which is hot and active."

"Right!" we all echoed and began to work with the blue construction paper.

"What shape should it be?" I asked.

"It could be a square," said one teacher.

"Why?" we asked.

"I don't know; it just feels square to me, like being in a room."

"No," another said, "I think it should be round."

"Why round?"

"Because it has no beginning or end. It just goes round and round back to the same place."

"Does it really come back to the same place? Are you at the same place after reflection as you were before you started?"

"Well, not exactly."

"How about a spiral?" someone else suggested.

"Yeah, a spiral has the qualities of the circle, but ends up in a different place from where it began."

"Yeah, that's it!" we all cried, and began to shape the spiral out of the blue paper.

At the annual Principals' Conference, Expeditionary Learning facilitators asked the principals to depict in a black-and-white collage a design principle that best represented their educational vision. Mark Weiss, principal of School for the Physical City, who picked Intimacy and Caring, sketched his role as a community adviser walking with a small group of students on New York's city blocks.

"Wait a minute," someone cried. "Is the spiral the reflection itself, or is it the thoughts that come out of reflection? What if we make reflection a blue circle and then have thoughts coming out of it in a spiral form?"

"What would the thoughts look like?"

"At first they would be crude, unformed, and then as they progress along the spiral they take more and more shape."

"Cool!"

Rafael Hernandez teacher Michelle A. Mejia sculpts a statue of a human body at the Bodies in Tune Summit. Photograph by Elizabeth Maynard.

We began to work on shaping the thoughts. "What shape should the final thought be?"

"I don't know, but it should represent all complete thoughts, not just one particular idea."

"How about a light bulb?"

"That's it," cried some.

"No, too corny," protested others. "It should be a shape that represents a finished thought."

"How about a star?"

"Yeah, a star!" Long threads of different colored paper, some twisted, some curled emerge from the deep blue. They gradually begin to take form and finally become a star at the end of the spiral.

"The blue needs to be covered," someone says. "It is too exposed. A person needs protection from outside distractions to really enter into solitude and reflection." Someone fashions a tent over the blue reflective space. Another plants a rough human form inside.

"Shall he have a body or just a head?"

"Body, but no hands. Hands represent activity. The hands must be kept outside the tent, or they will tempt reflection and solitude to get busy and do all the stuff that has to be done." Two roughly shaped hands that looked as much like wings as hands were glued onto the top of the tent.

When we had finished, other groups came over to look at our work and guess what principle it represented. They had fascinating interpretations, ideas that we had never imagined, all revealing different aspects of solitude and reflection. Each person was able to read his or her own thoughts and experiences into the shapes and colors we had designed.

◆ ◆ ◆

Struggling to make a picture out of an idea helped us to discern the heart of the concept and all its subtle veins and arteries.

◆ ◆ ◆

The artistic process had stimulated much thoughtful reflection. Struggling to make a picture out of an idea helped us to discern the heart of the concept and all its subtle veins and arteries. What pushed our understanding deeper was the continual stream of good questions. Why . . . ? What if . . . ? If that were true, what about . . . ? How does that fit with what we said before? The questions were the catalyst that drove us to the heart of understanding and guided the design of the image we constructed. There were no wrong or right answers, just different ideas supported more or less by imaginative thought, judged by the collective experience of the group. Thus, subjective experience reached toward objectivity through confirmation by the experience of others. Imagination strove toward truth in the light of consistency and reason. The challenge to create an artistic representation of a concept unlocked an understanding and appreciation of solitude and reflection that we could never have gained through thinking alone. ◆

Steven Levy teaches at the Bowman School in Lexington, Massachusetts and works as a consultant for Expeditionary Learning Outward Bound.

Rethinking the School Schedule:

A New Model Gives Teachers Time to Plan

Amy Mednick

Students have the benefit of the renewed energy of a teacher who has the opportunity for midweek planning, reflection, and regrouping.

—A handwritten note to the principal from the first-grade team at Jack Elementary School in Portland, Maine

Walking down the halls at Jack Elementary School on Wednesday afternoons, one has a sense of calm, focus, and quiet unusual in the active learning environment of Expeditionary Learning schools. In their classrooms, teachers are engaging either individually or in small teams in planning their learning expeditions, conferring about the details of implementing them, or discussing some aspect of portfolio assessment. At Jack the school day ends at 12:30 P.M. on Wednesdays to allow for two hours of intensive teacher planning time.

The students do not lose out. In fact, they actually have fifteen minutes more instructional time per week than they had last year. And while the teachers are planning, the students attend an extended day enrichment program coordinated by the Portland Parks and Recreation Department.

It sounds like a pipe dream, but Principal Myrt Collins said she thinks making time each week for teacher planning could work at any elementary school.

Jack Elementary had an incentive: The new elementary teachers' contract allows for 150 minutes of individual planning time attached to their lunch periods. The district allocated money for the schools to hire lunch aides to cover for teachers during their daily planning sessions. But Collins said that that would not have been in the best interest of Jack children. As a high-risk inner-city school with a rate of transience close to 50 percent and with 87 percent of the students receiving free or reduced-price lunches, she said students need the stability of one classroom teacher.

"We got together with our staff and identified the

It sounds like a pipe dream, but Principal Myrt Collins said she thinks making time each week for teacher planning could work at any elementary school.

benefits to restructuring our school week—one that would address issues of the contract, and, more importantly, would meet our children's needs and give the teachers quality planning time," Collins said.

The staff found a way to maintain instructional time while increasing time for planning.

But how does this work?

The school day officially starts at 8:45 A.M.—fifteen minutes earlier than in previous years. And lunch runs forty-five minutes instead of one hour.

The new Monday, Tuesday, Thursday, and Friday schedule:

- Children eat breakfast between 8:30 and 8:45 A.M.
- The morning session runs from 8:45 A.M. to noon
- Lunch is forty-five minutes
- The afternoon session runs from 12:45 P.M. to 3:00 P.M.

On Wednesdays the morning session runs from 8:45 A.M. to noon. Lunch—a bag lunch delivered to the classroom—is thirty minutes. While most students go home at 12:30 P.M. and return at 1:30 P.M., there is on-site daycare for the small number of students whose parents work. That leaves two hours on Wednesday afternoons for teacher planning time.

To meet the contract, Jack teachers have a remaining thirty minutes each week for individual lesson planning, which they schedule independently. According to Collins, teachers mainly use the time to work in teams to develop ideas, plan learning

◆ ◆ ◆

The Wednesday afternoon planning time has been invaluable in preparing for fieldwork, working on assessments, arranging for outside experts, and for making the midcourse corrections that are an inevitable part of learning expeditions.

—Jan Pelletier

◆ ◆ ◆

expeditions, set up portfolio systems, and organize field experiences. Teachers have more time to collaborate, explore ideas, and take responsibility for learning.

Jan Pelletier, a second-grade teacher at Jack, used Wednesday afternoons to revise the learning expedition on transportation, which she and her fellow second-grade teachers initially planned during a summer institute. "The Wednesday afternoon planning time has been invaluable in preparing for fieldwork, working on assessments, arranging for outside experts, and for making the midcourse corrections that are an inevitable part of learning expeditions."

Expeditionary Learning's Scott Hartl, who works with the Portland schools, said it has helped the teachers to have an intensive block of time for planning.

"We would deem it unprofessional for trial lawyers to spend all of their time in a courtroom and neglect preparing their cases, but that is exactly what we ask teachers to do," Hartl said. "In general as a profession, all of the time teachers devote to planning for teaching and learning has to be squeezed into afterschool hours."

Hartl also said the weekly planning period has proved invaluable for developing learning expeditions, which cannot be fully prepared in advance. If the teachers want to make changes in the middle of an expedition, they have time to do that.

Students have benefited, Collins said, from an improved curriculum and work level and more efficient use of instructional time. Also, there are fewer interruptions in the school day because parents often set up appointments for Wednesday afternoons. In addition, Jack Elementary used the money the

Horacio Fernandez, of the Rafael Hernandez School in Boston, rushes down the hallway on his way home for the day. Photograph by David Cornwell.

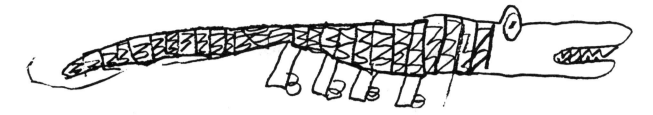

"The crocodile opens his jaws to scare his enemies," an illustration by Nathan Erickson, a second grader at Table Mound Elementary School in Dubuque, Iowa.

district had allocated for lunch aides to pay for the enrichment program. Most of the children, Collins said, would not have been able to afford activities such as ballet, pottery, theater, or hockey, which are some of the classes the enrichment program offers on Wednesday afternoons.

Much of the change required a more holistic view of how students learn, Collins said. For instance, she said she believes instructional time begins when students are preparing to come inside from recess. Teachers are using every moment—asking brain teasers as the students prepare to enter the building, she said.

Most important, she said, in order for this new system to work, the school community must agree and understand that students learn through social interaction as well as by improving cognitive skills.

"We've had the time to ask ourselves what is the image of the child for us, what is our image of learning, and how is knowledge constructed?" Collins said. "It's also given us some time to reflect and discover the whole realm of possibilities that are out there—all the lessons we can learn." ◆

Amy Mednick is the editor of The Web.

Part Six

Reflecting on Practice

I like that there is time given for solitude and reflection at the end of the day. It is very peaceful, it gives the child a chance to think about things, wind down, just kind of leave with peace within them- selves, instead of just gathering up bags and running out the door. My daughter, as a person, has grown.

—Parent

Academy for Educational Development Evaluation

Diversity and Inclusivity:
A Closer Look at Multicultural Curricula

Kim N. Archung

Diversity and inclusivity in all groups dramatically increases richness of ideas, creative power, problem-solving ability, and acceptance of others. Encourage students to investigate, value, and draw upon their own different histories, talents, and resources together with those of other communities and cultures. Keep schools and learning groups heterogeneous.

I think that the idea of diversity and inclusivity is noble. Teachers often address this idea by attempting to broaden students' knowledge about particular groups of people and their histories. We frequently do this by developing curricula focused on the study of a particular culture. We provide students with experiences that help them to explore the lives of members of that culture throughout history. We engage students in exciting projects and demonstrations, recreating artifacts that represent the cultural group. At times, cultural studies might also include authentic engagement with representatives from that particular cultural group.

Yet the idea of diversity and inclusivity makes me feel uncomfortable. I feel as if the words and their connotations circumvent a deeper, yet more unpleasant discussion. They seem to be euphemisms for the more complex and difficult issues of racism, ethnocentrism, and exclusion. These issues are the underlying reasons for engaging in the notions of diversity and inclusivity, but they pose a tension and discomfort that are not usually welcome conversation.

When I hear the words *diversity* and *inclusivity* used in educational discourse, I feel distressed as I wonder what this means for those who traditionally have been excluded. As the United States becomes increasingly more diverse, the need for its schools accurately to address issues of diversity and inclusivity also increases. "Multicultural" focuses in curricula and education have become a common trend in response to the demand to diversify and to make curriculum more inclusive. The publishing companies have capitalized on this growing trend: many textbooks and basals now include multicultural information and literature in their formats. For instance, history texts now contain more, general information about Africa or the Civil Rights movement. In addition, classroom curricula now include many more multicultural themes.

But what does diversity and inclusivity mean to teachers faced with educating children who come from cultures other than their own? What does diversity and inclusivity mean when we are teaching about cultures other than our own? As I think of this

> But what does diversity and inclusivity mean to teachers faced with educating children who come from cultures other than their own?

quandary, I am reminded of the powerful title of Lisa Delpit's book *Other People's Children.* Do we in fact think of children who come from varying cultural backgrounds as other people's children, or do we think of all children as our own? If we think of all children as our own, then would we not want their experiences in school and in the world to reflect a celebration of their cultures and familial experiences? Would we not want to ensure that their voices and perspectives are validated and honored? As a teacher, I am reminded that it is my responsibility to ensure these types of experiences by providing my students with many opportunities to examine critically the multiple perspectives within the variety of global cultures. Yet I must first look below the surface of general practices and traditional approaches to cultural studies.

Developing curriculum that speaks to issues of culture is often challenging and difficult. Culture is a complex concept. There are the obvious, explicit aspects of culture that most people recognize like food, clothing, shelter, music, dance, and art forms. However, the implicit characteristics of culture frequently get misplaced in discussions and explorations about people and their histories. These more complex aspects, such as belief systems, views of the world, ways of constructing knowledge, and historical perspectives, help to shape the very nature of those cultures. Quite often "multicultural" curriculum tends to miss these intangible qualities of culture, causing students and teachers to walk away from a cultural study with more of a misconception or exotic view of the people being studied than they might have had when they began. If we are truly to address "Diversity and Inclusivity," I feel that we need to focus on these issues more openly and directly, while examining, questioning, and critiquing what we know about racism and the role it plays in shaping our misconceptions of culture.

Below the Surface

As a teacher I encountered this challenge. In 1992 I was faced with the task of developing and teaching my multiage students (third through sixth graders) a curriculum that addressed the Columbus Quincentennial. I wanted my students to look at the quincentennial with critical eyes and to gain access to multiple perspectives of the "Columbus Story." I believed they should develop an awareness and understanding of the native people who first lived in the Americas. Therefore, I wanted my students to know something about the roots of Native American culture. More important, I expected to plant some seeds within my students' minds that would encourage and stimulate them to look below the surface of the stereotypes and their general knowledge about "Indians." In developing these skills, I also hoped my students would acquire some knowledge of the contributions and status of Native Americans in current events. In turn, I wanted them to know how the historical perspectives of the dominant culture have shaped our perceptions of "other" people, and in particular Native Americans. By developing an appreciation for various aspects of Native American culture, I wanted my students to learn about the impact of indigenous people in the history of the Americas.

I was faced with the challenge of trying to figure out the best focus for this curriculum as I had only general knowledge of Native Americans and limited knowledge of any one nation. In my third- through sixth-grade class, I integrated language arts, social studies, and art. I had always been focused on implementing experiential curricula much like learning expeditions. I therefore wanted my students to have hands-on, meaningful experiences while developing critical thinking skills.

My first task was somehow to break down the barriers of negative and stereotyped images that have influenced us all. I began by asking students to find information on Native American people. Each student brought in at least one book that de-

Most of the books' illustrations were caricatures, or cartoonlike. None of their information indicated anything about contemporary Native Americans.

picted Native Americans. I asked students to describe what they knew and had learned about "Indians" from their research.

Several of my third-grade students gleaned much of their information from movies or television. They shared many grossly generalized statements about Native Americans, such as "Indians live in teepees," or "Indians use bows and arrows." Most of the books' illustrations were caricatures, or cartoonlike. None of their information indicated anything about contemporary Native Americans. I do not think any of them found books with actual photographs.

After each student discussed at least one piece of information with the class, I began to write their generalizations in paragraph form on the board. I asked them to look at what we had written, and then I began to replace the word *Indians* with other nouns such as *Chinese*, *African Americans*, *Italians*, *Boys*, and *Girls*. Immediately the class noticed how bizarre and exaggerated their statements sounded. This exercise introduced the idea of stereotyping to my

I looked through a lot of books and found some examples of stereotypes. One of the books had a cartoon-like Indian dressed in a feather headdress. It also had a teepee. Not all Native Americans lived in teepees. Only some of them did like the Sioux. People need to be careful about books they read because they might have stereotypes.

Rafael Hernandez School fifth-grade student Melissa Ferreira completed this project on examining stereotypes for an expedition on Native Americans.

students. I pointed out to them that perhaps what we knew about Native Americans was limited and shaped by images depicted in books and films largely produced by people who were not Native American.

This opening exercise led us on a yearlong exploration of the people native to America. I built our exploration around historical research, which included examining multiple perspectives of the Columbus story by answering the questions "Who discovered America?" or "Where would we be if Columbus had never sailed the ocean blue?" Many of the questions emerged from the students' conversations and comments in class as they began to develop broader perspectives about "The People,"

which is how we began to refer to the many nations of Native Americans.

Further along in the year we delved into various literary styles of Native American writers, storytellers, and orators. We explored myth and poetry as well as examples of more contemporary writings. We integrated art into our work as we looked at the different forms of creative expression represented throughout the variety of Native American cultures. The project creating prayer sticks and learning their purpose engaged students the most. It helped them experience the meaning and use of art in the daily lives of native people, which in turn led us in search of uncovering the mysteries of Native Americans' connection to the earth and their spiritual beliefs.

I found the teacher resource *Through Indian Eyes: The Native Experience in Books for Children* invaluable. *Through Indian Eyes* critiques many of the commonly used books about Native Americans. The

◆ ◆ ◆

It was one thing to provide my students with creative and interesting ideas that I thought would help them to appreciate Native American culture, but it was another thing for me to teach them to value and to respect the multiplicity of perspectives in other people's stories.

voices of the Native Americans who edited this resource book provided authentic information. Those authentic voices, which guided me through classes focusing on certain literature selections, increased sensitivity. Many of the stories in the book received negative critiques, not because they weren't good stories but because they were historically and culturally incorrect. I was better able to provide information that helped the students look at the materials with a more critical eye. I learned the importance of including authentic voices and mul-

My picture is a stereotype toward Native Americans. It's a stereotype that the Native American is a violent attacker and the European is a helpless victim. Also, some Native Americans did dress in that way and lived in teepees, but it's a stereotype to think that they all did. All Native Americans didn't use bows and arrows. They all didn't use knives and peace pipes or talk in that way ("Me want scalp"). Probably most Native Americans didn't even scalp! Also, Native Americans shouldn't be called savages!

Anna Goodkind, a fifth grader at the Rafael Hernandez School in Boston, drew this image to convey typical stereotypes of Native Americans, and then she wrote about those distorted views.

tiple perspectives from the cultural group being explored. It was one thing to provide my students with creative and interesting ideas that I thought would help them to appreciate Native American culture, but it was another thing for me to teach them to value and to respect the multiplicity of perspectives in other people's stories. While a year seemed like a long time to focus on one topic, I found that it was not enough time to do justice to the exploration of Native American culture.

In my work with Expeditionary Learning Outward Bound, I have observed many learning expeditions that have issues of culture and diversity embedded within them. Teachers are developing learning expeditions on topics as broad as Native Americans, Africa, Egypt, Asia, and World Issues. Broadening

the perspectives of the students we teach while engaging them in intellectually challenging topics of study is one goal of implementing a learning expedition. Topics that are provocative and engaging are always powerful ways through which to deepen students' knowledge and understanding. Yet, I have also observed a need to pay attention to how these learning expeditions are shaped and implemented so that they do not become laden with subtle, yet significant, perpetuations of bias. I have been particularly struck by the common themes, projects, and outcomes of multicultural learning expeditions. Project ideas such as making feathered headdresses, dream catchers, teepees, masks, or pyramids can provide students with creative exercises and a window into understanding certain aspects of particular cultures. However, I question whether they reinforce stereotypes and give students an accurate and authentic understanding of the unique and rich expressions that exist within cultures. In other words, they may be first steps, but in my view, they are not sufficient unto themselves.

As Christine Sleeter points out in her article "White Racism" in *Multicultural Education* (Spring, 1994, p. 6.), "far too often the response is to experience other cultures as a tourist or colonist would." When we teach cultural studies this way, we explore culture in a vacuum and separate it from its historical and political perspectives. We create a mystique that reinforces preconceived notions and stereotypes. In doing so, we simplify the complexity of the cultural histories and global relationships of that particular culture. This can only tacitly reinforce notions of racism and white privilege, which are at the root of our need to diversify and make our educational processes more inclusive.

Rocky Mountain School of Expeditionary Learning (Denver) students Jackie Phillips and Lauren Rutherford compare their layout of bones to the skeleton during an expedition on the human body. Photograph by David Cornwell.

Shattering Stereotypes

In launching their learning expedition on Native Americans this year, fifth-grade teachers Eloise Biscoe and Wanda Muriel strove to find out what the students already knew about the people and the culture.

"Almost exclusively they drew an Indian running around the campfire with a teepee in the background," said Biscoe, who teaches at the Rafael Hernandez School in Boston. A few students, who had studied the Taino people from Puerto Rico the previous year, sketched less stereotypical housing. But most students had seen distorted images of Native Americans on television.

After that brief exercise, teachers began a conversation about stereotypes. The students looked through books for examples, and then discussed why they considered them stereotypes. Students selected novels with Native American themes, and learned to write critiques of the stereotypes found within the books.

"For example, if the book refers to simply Native Americans or Indians and a tribe is never mentioned, or if a character speaks pidgin English, we point these things out," Biscoe said.

Finally, the students pulled together their ideas in their "Present Day Projects" on Native American stereotyping, which included projects such as picking a stereotype found in a book and commenting on why it was a stereotype, or drawing a representation of a stereotype and describing it.

While the students seemed to come away from the expedition with an awareness of the history of Native Americans and a true feeling for the diversity of peoples within the culture, Biscoe still is not satisfied with the depth of their understanding of stereotypes.

"I always feel this is our weakest part of the expedition because it's tough to get at stereotypes," she said. In the future, Biscoe said she would like to concentrate more on stereotyping in general and delve into how the distorted images relate to the students' own lives. A simple exercise might include having students respond to open-ended statements such as "White people are . . . ," "African American people are . . . ," or "Hispanic people are . . ."

I have listened to teachers read stories, such as *The Indian in the Cupboard*, by Lynne Reid Banks, to their students with an enthusiasm that would suggest the story provides students with a qualitative

◆ ◆ ◆

Critically examining our own understandings of culture, racism, and ethnocentrism, as well as our attitudes toward those who may be considered "others," is a first step in growing toward a conscious awareness, recognition, and honest value of diversity and inclusivity.

◆ ◆ ◆

view of Native American culture. I would propose that teachers examine the idea of a Native American warrior being reduced to the level of a toy for its psychological and political implications. What underlying statement is being made when we sug-

gest an Indian warrior lives in a toy cupboard and has a vocabulary and dialogue that consists of "ughs" and broken English?

The exclusion of perspectives outside of the dominant culture from traditional educational practices has forced us to try to create a quick–fix situation called "multicultural education." The intention is noble in effort if it encourages a deeper appreciation for and celebration of the cultural diversity of our world. However, multicultural studies have a tendency to leave out the discourse about racism. As Christine Sleeter wrote, very often this focus is illustrated in ways that simplify and devalue others while rendering a European-centered perspective as invisible or normal. The focus is primarily on cultural differences. The point of view from which information is constructed about the particular culture is neither examined nor deeply questioned.

It takes courage to be aware of the many ways in which cultural bias and insensitivity are perpetuated. Teachers and students, however, must gain an authentic sense of the people and cultures under study. Critically examining our own understandings of culture, racism, and ethnocentrism, as well as our attitudes toward those who may be considered "others," is a first step in growing toward a conscious awareness, recognition, and honest value of diversity and inclusivity.

I firmly believe that unless we are willing to have the more difficult conversations about the reasons

Virginia Dunn, a teacher at the Rafael Hernandez School in Boston, explains the lifecycle of a chick to her first-grade class. Photograph by David Cornwell.

Selected Resources

The Anti-bias Curriculum. Five videocassettes published by Educational Technology Department, CUNY, Cobleskill, N.Y., 1990. Tel.: (518) 234-5841.

Darder, Antonio. *Culture and Power in the Classroom: A Critical Foundation for Bicultural Education.* New York: Bergen and Garvey, 1991.

Delpit, Lisa. *Other People's Children: Cultural Conflict in the Classroom.* New York: New Press, 1995.

Slapin, Beverly, and Seale, Doris, eds. *Through Indian Eyes: The Native Experience in Books for Children.* Philadelphia: New Society Publishers, 1992. Tel.: (800) 333-9093.

Organizations

Primary Source offers professional development and curriculum resources on multicultural and global education for teachers and school communities. Address: P.O. Box 381711, Cambridge, MA 02238; (617) 661-8832; primary@ace.com.

Facing History and Ourselves offers teacher training designed to engage students in an examination of racism, prejudice, and anti–Semitism by using the historical example of the Holocaust to help students make the connection between history and the moral choices confronted in their own lives. Address: 16 Hurd Street, Brookline, MA 02146; (617) 232-1595.

why we have a need to create "multicultural" curriculum, we will only continue to water down these efforts with surface information that continues to exclude an integration of multiple perspectives, stories, and truths. If we are truly to honor and to practice this design principle, which suggests the need to collaborate in building a cultural democracy, we need to commit to engaging in multifaceted explorations. In a cultural democracy, all peoples' belief systems, views of the world, ways of constructing knowledge, and historical perspectives are valued and honored. Culturally democratic practices include a critical analysis of how racism and its effects have structured our lives, viewpoints, vested interests, and daily actions. We must engage in a dialogue that includes multiple perspectives from individuals who represent the cultures being studied. We can stretch our own and our students' views as we build a knowledge base by critically examining the available information and by searching deeply for additional knowledge. When we make the commitment to screen for stereotypes and ask questions such as "Whose history is being told here?" and "How and where can I find out more information?" and then teach students the skills of how to do these things for themselves, we will truly foster diversity and inclusivity. ◆

Kim N. Archung is a school designer with Expeditionary Learning Outward Bound.

Celebration and Critique

Leah Rugen

The sunny conference room falls silent as the group of faculty thinks and writes intently. Asked to consider how their summer learning expedition plans have changed and evolved over the course of the fall, they lean over notebooks in concentration. A few sighs are heard.

Expeditionary Learning Outward Bound staff and teachers use the word *reflection* a great deal. The ninth design principle, Solitude and Reflection, asks that we "be sure students have time alone to explore their own thoughts, make their own connections, and create their own ideas." We also talk about teachers reflecting on their practice and on students' learning, but what does that actually mean? How does it work? Why is it important?

In New York, San Antonio, and Portland, Maine, formal staff development days scheduled in the fall of 1995 have fostered reflection on learning expeditions. Within a structured format, teachers have gathered as teams and whole faculties to celebrate their successes and to venture into the riskier territory of self- and peer-critique.

Examining their learning goals for learning expeditions and considering the work their students produced, teachers have asked themselves and each

◆ ◆ ◆

In order to improve their practice and push their students to higher achievement, teachers must be open to doubt.

◆ ◆ ◆

other questions: "What are students learning, *really*? What lessons can I apply to my next learning expedition? How can I keep improving as a teacher?" Such questions, grappled with during these reflection days, bridge the gap between curriculum and assessment. They invite teachers to look closely both at what students have learned and produced, and at their own design and teaching of the learning expedition.

In *Teaching, Making Sense of an Uncertain Craft* (Teachers College Press, 1992), Joseph McDonald describes teaching as a balance between doubt and belief. In order to guide their students successfully, teachers must maintain a strong core of belief in

The AV Squad: Sam Schwartz, former New York City traffic commissioner, and a student check out traffic radar equipment. Photograph by Carrie Boretz for the New York Times.

themselves and their students. But in order to improve their practice and push their students to higher achievement, teachers must be open to doubt. This work, with its doubt and self-reflection, can be lonely. But in the company of colleagues and within a forum structured to provide support as well as feedback, doubt and self-reflection can be dynamic and motivating. The process is still not easy, but it is no longer lonely.

After a day spent writing and talking with peers, Marianne Melendez, a humanities teacher at School for the Physical City in New York, conveyed the value of structured reflection in a message to her colleagues on the school's E-mail conference:

I came away from yesterday's meeting with tremendous self-doubt and confusion about a particular humanities class. I have struggled since the beginning of the year with it. So I listened to myself all night, and to all of you (your ideas, responses, struggles). Today, I took a risk and told my students that I saw a problem with two interrelated parts. I invited responses, and we set a short-term agenda. The students and I then took up a thread from the learning expedition that we had abandoned too quickly earlier. The class went very well, and my faith in my students and, dare I say, in myself is renewed. Even my homework assignment felt well-structured and clearly related . . . nary a groan was heard. Thank you . . . all of you . . .

Will Pidden, a technology-arts teacher at King Middle School in Portland, Maine, asked a group of colleagues to help him think through a dilemma in his teaching. Describing and demonstrating a long-term project in which students designed working models of carnival rides, Pidden explained his question: "I see them in class figuring a lot of things out, but the final product is hard to judge. How can I have kids record and present their thinking? How can I help them recognize what they have learned?" Over the course of a half hour, a group of Pidden's colleagues followed a protocol in which they asked questions, offered warm support for his work, and then gave thoughtful responses to his question.

The faculties of two elementary schools in San Antonio, Texas, implementing Expeditionary Learning for the first time, gathered for a daylong conference focused on reflecting on learning expeditions.

Having just experienced the roller coaster ride of implementing their first learning expeditions, the two faculties presented the best examples of students' project work in a morning gallery. Then, as the day progressed, they reflected more deeply on the work they saw and their own experience during their expeditions. After some individual writing and reflection, small work groups developed written guidelines for planning and implementing strong learning expeditions.

"I think that what we're doing is something totally different," said Guadalupe Ruvalcaba, who serves as a school designer based in San Antonio. "Rather than just delivering professional development, we're building the capacity of the faculties by teaching them to critique each other's work. At the same time, we're providing a safety net in that everyone is participating together."

Excerpts from Teachers' Journals: Reflections on Learning Expeditions in San Antonio

I learned if you expect these wonderful ideas from the children, they will produce wonderful projects. I also learned that these projects must be planned well in order for them to have such a good outcome.

I was afraid to let students take charge of all of the steps involved with making a life-size Flat Stanley [a boy represented in a book who grows up flat] to scale. I let students go and they did it! From this I learned that I have been holding them back in not letting them do other things completely on their own.

The first bright moment was when we went on our first community walk. The students were so excited to show me their houses, where they play, and who their neighbors were. It was also an opportunity for me to see their community through their eyes. The students put a story to the buildings and houses I so carelessly pass by every day.

Throughout the expedition the students have written books. The students have steadily become independent writers. They show such pride in their finished products that they now want to share with all. Confidence is high.

Piloted in San Antonio by Herff and Douglas elementary schools, similar days are scheduled for the other Expeditionary Learning Outward Bound schools in San Antonio.

In the following interview, Expeditionary Learning Outward Bound school designer Scott Hartl

◆ ◆ ◆

We ask teachers to roll up their sleeves and jump in immediately and design curriculum in a form that's very new to most of them— the learning expedition.

—Scott Hartl

◆ ◆ ◆

discusses some of the lessons of a day that grew out of a close collaboration with Cambridge colleagues Leah Rugen, Denis Udall, and Kathy Greeley, and with San Antonio colleagues Guadalupe Ruvalcaba, Douglas Elementary Principal Sylvia Garza, and Herff Elementary Principal Mary Helen Rodriguez.

How did this day come about? Isn't it unusual for a new school to undertake this level of reflection during their first year?

What's great is that it didn't have to do with me at all. During the Expeditionary Learning leadership retreat this summer, the schools' two superb principals, Sylvia Garza and Mary Helen Rodriguez, had the intuition and forethought to schedule two reflection days during the year as part of their professional development plans, one after the first learning expedition and the second at the end of the year. The two schools are "sisters": Herff is pre-K through grade two, and all of the students attend Douglas for grades three to five. They do a great deal of professional development as joint faculties. I quickly saw the power of their ideas and went about designing the day.

What were your collective goals for the day, and why is this kind of day important?

Reflection is such a critical part of Expeditionary Learning's professional development sequence. Unlike some other school change models, we ask teachers to roll up their sleeves and jump in immediately and design curriculum in a form that's very new to most of them—the learning expedition. Because of this experiential approach, it's critical to pause at several points in the year to mine the learning from experience.

Three students examine kelp held up by Tim Cronin, a science teacher at King Middle School in Portland, Maine, for the learning expedition "The Ocean: What's Under There?" Photograph by David Cornwell.

Reading together, David Schwartz, Gregory Benoit, and Brandon Maryland, students at the Rafael Hernandez School in Boston, uncover the classic children's storybook Charlotte's Web, *by E.B. White. Photograph by David Cornwell.*

We had three goals. The first was to take the time to share and celebrate the work that was done in the first eighteen weeks of school. That just doesn't happen in the fast-paced week-to-week existence of schools. So we wanted to allow teachers to know what everyone had accomplished and to celebrate it. The second goal was to begin the process of self- and peer-reflection and critique. We wanted to come out of the day with a document that would be a self-generated set of criteria for planning learning expeditions, and that captured what the two faculties had learned from planning and implementing their first. Finally, the day centered on building a sense of ownership.

The kind of changes that teachers are being asked to make through Expeditionary Learning are both wide and deep. It was important to acknowledge that teachers were still questioning and wondering if they could own this style of teaching and learning. One of the most powerful ways to help the ownership grow is to ask people to share their work and articulate what they have learned.

Would you talk a little about the structure of the day and the importance of structure?

Sharing your work is an intimidating process for anyone. Although there are many experienced and even master-level teachers in both schools, there was a pervasive feeling of discomfort and anxiety about sharing work. So having a solid structure through which teachers share and critique work was critical to keeping the process safe.

We started with the celebration first. As teachers explored the gallery of student work, they were asked to write specific positive comments about what they saw and to post those comments on a wall. At the end of the gallery, we collected the comments and read them aloud. It took a solid ten minutes. That set us off on a positive foot for the day. In order for people to have the trust and relationships to hear and respond to constructive comments, there has to be a background of a lot of positive support. It seems so simple, but it's a step that is often skipped or slighted.

Another key element of the structure was that people were active. There were very few moments in which people listened to a facilitator's comments. Instead, almost all of the agenda involved teachers looking at each other's work, reflecting on their own experiences, or working in small groups. We really wanted to cultivate a sense that this was their day. Rather than looking for experts, teachers felt validated that they possessed the answers collectively. The role of Expeditionary Learning was to facilitate a process that helped the teachers dig deeply into their experiences and come up with a common document of their ideas and lessons. They felt invigorated by that.

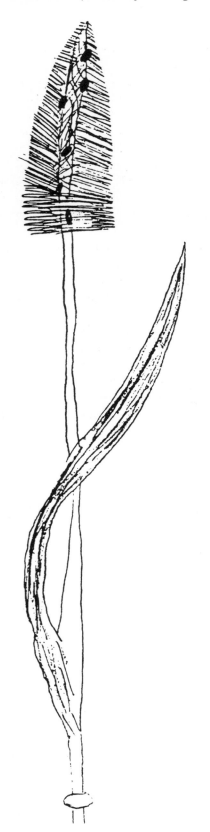

Giant Yellow Fox Tail by sixth-grade student Jennifer Hoffmann for the learning expedition "Do You See What I See?" at Table Mound Elementary School in Dubuque, Iowa.

How does individual reflection and the use of journal writing fit into the process?

I think that individual reflective writing is often our most accurate window into teachers' true experiences. In small-group conversations, sometimes the more difficult feedback doesn't emerge. Reflective writing doesn't just help people to capture meaning that they have already built; it helps them build larger meaning. Writing also creates a quality of time different from that which teachers typically have. Very rarely do teachers have the opportunity to be silent and reflective.

Actually, the journal was the glue of the day. Teachers were asked questions for every session, and the journals became both a reflective tool for the teacher and part of the whole group's material for documentation. In effect there were two information-gathering segments, the gallery and the

◆ ◆ ◆

I think that individual reflective writing is often our most accurate window into teachers' true experiences.

—Scott Hartl

◆ ◆ ◆

individual writing. Teachers then spent the rest of the day in small groups to work through the elements of the learning expedition framework and capture what they learned about each area.

How did it help to have the student work to refer to throughout the day?

Expeditionary Learning can feel very abstract. Student work grounds the design and allows the teachers to talk about difficult and abstract principles in concrete terms. There is also something honoring about holding up the work of students. It allows us to look at the process of teaching and learning, and the teacher's role, through tangible evidence of student learning.

Lined Seahorse (Hippacampus erectus).

General Physical Description: A Lined Seahorse has a horselike head, a long tail, and a fin on its back. It can change its color. Its size ranges from 5 centimeters to 13 centimeters. It has a big appetite. The seahorse can watch predators with one eye and prey with the other. Their eyes independently achieve binocular vision.

Habitat: Seahorses live in mangroves, sea grass, and coral reefs (shallow waters).

Food Eaten: They eat minute planktonic crustaceans. They have a small mouth at the end of long, tubelike snouts. The food is eaten by a rapid intake of water.

Role in the Food Chain: Their predators are mollusks, crabs, penguins, and fish.

Reproductive Life: The males get pregnant constantly from October to April. The female puts her eggs into a pouch that the male has at the top of his tail. The eggs are incubated for ten days. There are often over 1,000 eggs. The labor lasts for ten days, and the father will eat some of the offspring. All offspring are one-quarter to one-half inch in length.

Interactions in Its Community: Newcomers to their community are taken in almost immediately.

Human Interactions: Seahorses are kept in aquariums and studied in the ocean. They are also sold and eaten around the world.

Geographic Range: Seahorses live in North and South America, Europe, Africa, Asia, the Bahamas, Mexico, and Australia. The Lined Seahorse is found from Nova Scotia to Argentina.

Status: Current research indicates that their life span is unknown, but scientists believe their population is threatened. There is a trade for dead or living seahorses, and top prices are paid for them all over the world. They are caught and sold to other countries. Pollution is ruining their homes, and people are using them for medicines. Humans are destroying their habitat.

Illustration of Lined Seahorse by Joel McIlwain, a seventh-grade student at King Middle School, for the field guide "The Ocean: What's Under There?"

So what were some of the lessons teachers gleaned from implementing their summer plans?

They discovered that some projects planned were too grandiose. They hadn't taken into account that it was the beginning of the year. Often the practicalities and details only became clear after they started into the learning expedition. Almost universally, people realized they needed to give the expedition more time. I thought it was wonderful how many comments centered on strategies like rehearsing, practicing, drafting, and providing good models. People realized that such strategies made or broke the quality of what students produced.

Everyone was amazed at the difference between plan and reality. But they were very proud of the work and excited to plan another expedition. The original expectations for these schools were that they would develop two learning expeditions over the course of the year. A large number of teachers are on their way toward completing a second learning expedition before Christmas, far exceeding this expectation. Some have even planned three. There is a real sense of positive momentum. ◆

Leah Rugen is the associate director of Expeditionary Learning.

Homework?
What Homework?
Achieving Excellence
without Tears

Loretta Brady, with help from School for the
Physical City students

I had just learned to rollerblade—thought I was pretty good too—when I found myself racing out of control down the slope at Fifty-ninth and First. Aiming for something to break my fall, I grabbed hold of a skinny little tree and began twirling, lassolike, about its slender trunk until the inevitable crash. The concrete bit through my sleeve and scraped my flesh in places they don't make protective padding for.

I learned a thing or two. I wasn't as good as I thought I was. I also vowed that with a little more practice I would master the downhills one day.

Nicole Kangas, a seventh grader at King Middle School in Portland, Maine, drew the Green Sea Urchin for the field guide as part of the Casco Bay learning expedition.

Reprinted from *Parent Perspectives: The Newsletter of the School for the Physical City Family School Partnership Communications Committee* 2:2 (Nov. 1994).

Wouldn't it be great if the drive to do excellent work were as gripping for students as it is for in-line skaters? Imagine if kids loved the struggle of intellectual achievement as much as they love to skate? You'd never hear School for the Physical City (SPC) staff and families saying, "What do you mean you have nothing to do now? You *know* you get rollerblading in every subject every night; now lace up!"

High-level habits of mind come only through regular nightly practice.

Well, the fact remains, it is a struggle. Despite new approaches toward more purposeful, creative, and personalized assignments, truly excellent accomplishments will take sweat and sometimes a few scrapes.

SPC and other good schools know that the best goal is to have students own the desire for excellence. Ultimately, students must accept the responsibility to get themselves organized, focused, and truly thoughtful about meaningful work.

Sound serious? Yes. No pain, no gain.

High-level habits of mind come only through regular nightly practice. Every study we read tells us again and again that the gap between those who are excellent and those who are not is much more a matter of time than of talent.

Sound dull? Is rollerblading dull? Besides, since assignments are somewhat open-ended, students can shape their work to fit their level of challenge, or to suit their passion.

SPC requests and demands that each child complete nightly responsibilities and develop habits for excellent learning. Children should carry their monthly independent reading book all the time. They should do about thirty minutes of quality reading and studying in each subject each night. (Humanities is two subjects.) In seminars and reading groups, we have a rule that you can't participate if you have not prepared your reading notes. More and more, we are showing children models of excellent student work, as we ask them to self-critique and redo their work accordingly.

146

LEAF 1⅛ inches

RINGS—6

CIRCUMFERENCE — 1¼ inches

Artwork by Cal Follman, a student at Central Alternative High School in Dubuque, Iowa, for the "Natural Reflections" learning expedition.

Students at the School for the Physical City in New York give their answers to the question "What are some of the most helpful or meaningful homework assignments you value?"

When I asked my dad about activities he respects.

—Stanley Takaro

Making my own robot.

—Brooke Lastra

Just reading your own book.

—Macky Bergman-Clark, Michael Williams

Doing writing revision, especially on computers.

—Dwight Monroe

Making a book about kites and air.

—Maishia Gilman, Asad Beldo

When we're assigned xeroxes from parts of books. This way we read important parts of many different books—and now I want to read one of them.

—Margaret Cassanova

We are asking Community Circle leaders to act as advisers and contact families whenever homework responsibilities are sliding. We have sent home "it's-not-too-late-to-succeed" notes to allow students to improve before the first report card. Parents need to sign these notes after students have filled in their plan of action section.

Nothing is more valuable than family input. You know best if your child is rollerblading at a level that is too easy or too difficult for her. Your child's Community Circle leader is your home base for working out strategies and solutions. Some families request mandatory after-school tutoring. Some ask to see student work folders or receive teacher correspondence regularly. Sometimes we agree to withhold privileges, the consequence for a child's neglect of duty.

This is a school that cares and listens. We want to know if your in-line skater is sitting too much on the bench or heading for injury. Most of all, we strive to make the responsibility of excellent skating the job of the skater. ◆

Loretta Brady is a humanities instructor at the School for the Physical City in New York.

Teacher Appraisal:

Getting It Right

Phil Gonring and Denis Udall

It is an all too familiar scene. The school principal or department chair arrives unannounced at your classroom door, clipboard in hand. She makes her way to the back of the room and for the next half hour scribbles notes, looking up every now and then to observe your lesson. Weeks later you find a form in your cubby with a brief written evaluation and a few boxes checked off. Perhaps you've been lucky enough to receive a few words of encouragement or praise. You are left asking, "Did she really take the time to understand me *as a teacher*?"

The Rocky Mountain School of Expeditionary Learning (RMSEL) in Denver has turned traditional teacher appraisal on its head: at RMSEL teacher evaluation revolves around adult development. Through a combination of letter writing, videotaping, classroom observation, and peer critique, teachers are assisting each other to reflect on their craft in ways that help them to do it better.

Research tells us that traditional teacher evaluation systems are largely ineffective. Evaluation is rarely linked with professional development, and in many cases it undermines teacher growth rather than enhancing it.

While many districts identify minimum competency standards or "effective teacher behaviors," few have the capacity or a process to assist teachers in improving their practice. Yet a number of studies have shown that accountability systems must do more than merely identify minimum competence; they need to foster a "climate of improvement through reflection (recognition of potential areas of growth) and the motivation to change," according to

Michael Fullan, in his book *The New Meaning of Educational Change*. A minor but important part of any system is what happens to teachers who get negative feedback but do not display improvement.

In short, the best systems are oriented toward and support teachers' development and improvement, where the overall environment is positive and supportive and is geared toward nurturing excellent performance. Such a system encourages teachers to

> Through a combination of letter writing, videotaping, classroom observation, and peer critique, teachers are assisting each other to reflect on their craft in ways that help them to do it better.

confront the complexities of their craft through observing, analyzing, and discussing among themselves and with their supervisors.

At RMSEL, teachers submit letters to their appraisal team discussing what they hope to be the focus of their appraisals. The appraisal team consists of a peer, a lead administrator, and the appraised teacher. (RMSEL does not have a principal. It has a lead administrative team composed of two teachers and a business manager.) The letters must address what the staff has identified as their three key concerns: instructional strategies, teaching and learning environment, and professionalism. The latter refers to the teacher's role as a member of the faculty and of a larger community that includes students, parents, and the school's governance council. The letter may contain the teacher's goals, fears, and concerns about his own teaching, what the appraisal team should look for during its observations, how the appraisal team might help the teacher, as well as challenges and accomplishments the teacher wants to accentuate.

Here are several excerpts from a letter written by kindergarten teacher Peter Thulson to his appraisers Steven Mercer, a third- and fourth-grade teacher, and Phil Gonring, one of RMSEL's lead teachers:

Dear Steven and Phil:

I'm eager for your help as I clarify and improve my work with students, parents, and colleagues. I see conventional templates for teacher practice and evaluation being broken here and ask that you focus on what I do rather than on what I'm not doing [emphasis added]. Help me see clearly what I'm doing now, help me refine my future goals, and help me find a route from one to the other.

The teacher then describes three areas of teaching he would like to improve, and elaborates on the second—documenting children's thinking and development (instructional strategies):

When I visited the Reggio Emilia schools in Italy in the fall, I was struck most of all by the importance the teachers there gave documentation. They connected it with a constructivist approach to learning and to a view of children as "protagonists." Documentation seemed at first to take far more of every teacher's time than instruction. Gradually, I realized it did take (and deserved) more time than instruction in my conventional sense of a distinct and teacher-centered attempt to transfer knowledge from an adult's skull to a child's. Documentation in Reggio was not distinguished from instruction . . .

◆ ◆ ◆

The correspondence undoes the standard and often destructive psychology surrounding teacher appraisal. In short, it makes it less threatening.

◆ ◆ ◆

. . . I've begun with three strategies [that are] in need of refinement. First, I began to meet with [my fellow team members] once a week to study our students' work. My models were the Reggio teachers honoring a child's scrawls by arguing like art or literary critics over rival hypotheses of what that child was up to.

Our sessions have been rich from the beginning. They are already the most valuable professional development experiences of my career. My goal is to notice more in students' work, to become more expert in seeing what is there and what it tells me about my students and their growth and how I might be of help to them . . .

The teacher goes on to talk about the difficulties he has had documenting student work and how he has recorded and transcribed student conversations.

The teacher's narrative helps appraisers understand how his practice has evolved over time and sets a clear context for three very specific goals: to notice more in student work, to become more expert in seeing what is in the work and consequently in students' minds, and to understand better how he might further their thinking. Clearer understandings

Science teacher Tim Cronin helps a King Middle School (Portland, Maine) student adjust his mask in preparation for entering the water. Photograph by David Cornwell.

Alisha Black Mallon, Anne Andrew, and Jessica Chase, students at Rocky Mountain School of Expeditionary Learning, take measurements of a small Denver river in preparation for studying the Mississippi River on a visit to Expeditionary Learning schools in Dubuque, Iowa. Photograph by David Cornwell.

of the teacher's practice also emerge for the appraiser through the process of writing a narrative about the observations along with an analysis of the account. Writing forces the appraiser to sit down and take the time to think about a teacher's practice.

The correspondence undoes the standard and often destructive psychology surrounding teacher appraisal. In short, it makes it less threatening. A letter addressed to Mercer and Gonring, two critical friends, takes the place of mysterious criteria and checklists.

Keeping in mind the areas of practice that the teacher requested that his appraisal team focus on, the team then observes four lessons, one of which is videotaped. Afterward, the appraisal team meets to analyze the videotape and the observed lessons. Then, each member of the appraisal team writes a letter in response to the observations and analysis of the videotape. Their letters address the appraised teacher's letter as well as other standards for teacher performance that might not have been included. The response includes praise as well as specific recommendations to support the teacher's growth. The teacher writes a second letter addressing these comments.

After reviewing these letters, the supervisor writes a final letter paying special attention to each of the three major roles of the teacher and makes specific recommendations for areas of growth. If necessary, the supervisor determines that the teacher needs to improve, setting in motion any requisite support and, if necessary, the process of termination.

This appraisal system is not without its costs. It requires a significant time commitment and a willingness on the part of teachers and administrators to reflect on and document the practice of teaching. But RMSEL's experiences have taught us that the investment pays off. The appraisal system forces us to focus our attention where it belongs: improving and reflecting on teaching and learning. By requiring a deep level of thought, analysis, and revision, it respects the complexity and subtlety of good teaching. ◆

Phil Gonring is a former lead team member at the Rocky Mountain School of Expeditionary Learning in Denver. Denis Udall is a school designer with Expeditionary Learning Outward Bound.

Collaborative Critique:
A Format for Teacher–to–Teacher Feedback

Denis Udall

Teachers at several Expeditionary Learning Outward Bound schools meet regularly for structured peer-to-peer feedback sessions called collaborative critiques. Adapted from the Coalition of Essential Schools' Tuning Protocol,[*] collaborative critique varies in format and content. Sometimes teachers present their learning expedition plans while at other times they share student project work. However, most of the sessions have several elements in common.

Each begins with the facilitator—usually another staff member—setting time limits and reminding participants of ground rules, such as be respectful, specific, and constructive, and begin with positive feedback before moving on to suggestions for improvement. Next, the teacher or team presents the context and background for the student work or the learning expedition plan. They might also pose a question or problem for the group to consider. This is followed by participants' clarifying questions.

Now the heart of the critique begins. Participants provide both "warm" and "cool" feedback while the presenters remain silent. Next it's the presenters' turn. They choose which comments or question to respond to, while the participants listen silently. Finally, the session ends with participants and presenters airing positive reactions, frustrations, or concerns.

Our early experience suggests that collaborative critique encourages faculties to view teacher practice and schoolwide learning goals and standards as intertwined. Each can inform the other. By inviting an individual teacher to reflect on and assess his or her practice in the company of peers, a school community becomes clearer about what it values in good teaching and high-quality student work.

The following is an interview with Peter Thulson and David Cornwell, teachers at Denver's Rocky Mountain School of Expeditionary Learning, about the process of presenting their learning expedition plans to their peers.

Dubuque teachers Diane Pancratz, Margaret Dettman, Kris Hermsen, Marcia Davis, Joan Connolly, and Becky Lorenzen take time away from school to plan their learning expeditions cooperatively. Photograph by David Guralnick.

When it was all over, how did you feel about the experience?

Cornwell: It was really affirming. It was so valuable to share my practice and my thinking with my colleagues. It was also frightening at first. But I came away from the session feeling honored to be part of a faculty where there's structural support for collegiality.

> It was also frightening at first. But I came away from the session feeling honored to be part of a faculty where there's structural support for collegiality.
>
> —David Cornwell

Thulson: It was very frightening and intimidating. Especially considering this was only the second time we had had a peer critique session as a faculty. It was particularly heroic of David, because he went first!

Sometimes it's hard to let go of the way faculty meetings are typically run and the kinds of things we discuss. But overall I found this to be a wonderful way for the faculty to spend time together, rather than just hammering out the lunch schedule or addressing discipline issues.

Why put yourself through this process if you were so anxious about it? I mean here's a situation that's potentially very threatening. You're really opening yourself up.

Cornwell: [Laughing] The fear of being found out!

Thulson: Some time ago I decided one of my personal goals was to put myself into positions that I might feel uncomfortable with—to go ahead and take the leap, even if I'm shaking.

The session was highly structured, partly, I think, as a way to manage the risks involved. At first it

felt a bit odd. As a faculty we're not accustomed to operating like that—"six minutes for the first segment, ten minutes for the next; you can speak during this time but not later on . . ." But I think it helped to reduce the anxiety. We're wandering into new territory, and it's nice to have a structure and have things be predictable.

Cornwell: One of the biggest challenges we have as a school is coming to terms with what we aspire to be as educators and human beings in contrast with where we are at this moment in time. You have to enter into a critique session in the faith that your colleagues will accept you as a human being who has aspirations that you're striving toward—ones that are noble and good. But there's still a lot of nervousness that comes with saying, "Hey, I'm incomplete in this area, but this is what I aspire to be, and this is how I'm trying to get there." Of course, every learner faces this struggle, whether you're a third grader or an adult.

A phrase we use a lot in my class is, how do you make something beautiful? It could be a piece of writing or the way you behave toward others—in other words, social or academic. This question ties together everything we do—everyone makes mistakes, but what can we do to make it right?

I'm struck that it's not just a matter of mistakes, but being respectful of what you—as a practitioner—don't know. Eleanor Duckworth writes about the "virtues of not knowing." All too often we skip over what we don't know. We rarely pause and contemplate the places where our understanding leaves off. Is this what you're speaking to—the need to reflect on and respect the messiness of one's practice?

Cornwell: I strongly believe in what I call approximations. I have a general idea of what I aspire to be and the steps I'm taking to achieve it. What's important is that I'm always growing in this direction. Now what happens if I don't meet the standard I've set for myself? If I don't get it right today, is that the end? Do I fail? No, as learner I reflect on it and come back tomorrow and make an approximation that's a little or a lot closer to where I want to go. This is an important concept for learners to have. The interesting thing is that the closer your approximations are to your original aspiration, the more you come to realize your aspirations have moved forward.

How did the session start? What did you do to focus your colleagues' attention?

Cornwell: I started by asking them a question—a kind of lens they could look at my learning expedition through. My question was, how does my expedition fit into an expeditionary framework, and the large school culture that we aspire to?

Collaborative Critique Suggested Format

I. Introduction (five minutes)
- Facilitator reminds participants of ground rules and sets time limits for discussion

II. Teacher Presentation (ten minutes)
- Teacher presents context for student work and/or learning expedition plans, including samples of student work and a question or problem she would like group to focus on

III. Clarifying Questions (five minutes)
- Participants ask background questions for clarification purposes only

IV. Sharing Feedback (fifteen minutes)
- Participants provide feedback, beginning with positive before moving on to suggestions for improvement
- Teacher-presenter remains silent

V. Presenter's Response (fifteen minutes)
- Teacher-presenter responds to those questions and comments she wishes to address
- Participants are silent

VI. Reflection (ten minutes)
- Time for airing frustrations, misunderstandings, or positive reactions participants may have experienced
- Invite participants to write about what they learned about their own practice as a result of the session

Adapted from the Coalition for Essential Schools' Tuning Protocol.

Thulson: The question I asked to guide their feedback was similar to David's, but I thought it could have had a tighter focus. I asked, where does my expedition plan fit, and where does it not fit your understanding of what a learning expedition is supposed to look like? It's a question that isn't resolved in the minds of our faculty, so it fed both ways. It became an opportunity for me to get feedback on my expedition, and for us as a faculty to have a conversation about what we mean by a learning expedition.

So the discussion produced good information on how to design an expedition, as well as being an opportunity for the entire community to define for itself what an expedition is?

Thulson: Yes. It was also useful to have that bigger conversation around specific examples, so we could say, this is what it is, and this is what it's not. It helped us to define further what Expeditionary Learning is and what instruction looks like within that framework.

Was there anything in particular that your colleagues said that you found helpful?

Thulson: They commented on how ambitious my plan was, but a few people were worried I didn't have adequate support for the children to complete our major project: a natural history guide to a park we're studying. During the critique session it helped me to hear my colleagues say, "I don't see in your learning expedition write-up how you're going to provide this level of support." Their comments encouraged me to think about the challenge I have ahead of me to keep track of all this material. ◆

---

* For more information see "The Tuning Protocol: A Process for Reflection," by David Allen, Coalition of Essential Schools, Brown University, February, 1995.

Denis Udall is a school designer with Expeditionary Learning Outward Bound.

Ocean Beds of Memory

Meg Campbell

Visiting schools often stirs memories of my own education in public kindergarten and junior high, parochial elementary, and a girls' Episcopal high school. The parochial stretch was the most tedious, yet in one significant way it cultivated and developed my visual intelligence.

The ingredients were simple: copies of great works of art coupled with simple projects that invited further study of them. Every year, each Friday afternoon the teacher handed us each a postcard reproduction, and read aloud from the art program guide about that week's project.

◆ ◆ ◆

One time we reproduced a Cézanne landscape in collage form using different kinds of dried noodles—dried macaroni made nice arches for Roman aqueducts.

◆ ◆ ◆

In first grade, when Sister Maria Dominga handed me Marc Chagall's whimsical, colorful *I and the Village*, I was transfixed. I barely listened to her description:

The man with the green face and the cow are staring at each other. It appears from the image of the milkmaid milking a cow, superimposed onto the cow's face, that the cow is thinking about being milked. Notice that the painting is very dreamlike and the colors used—pink, blue, green, white, orange—are not realistic but suggest a mood of wonder. This is a painting about memories of childhood.

She then asked us to make our own drawing of dreamlike scenes from our childhood. With my crayons and my small postcard of the painting, a new world opened to me. A world worth feasting upon and storing. I have that Chagall postcard before me as I write today.

One time we reproduced a Cézanne landscape in collage form using different kinds of dried noodles—dried macaroni made nice arches for Roman aqueducts. We matched the pattern of a Navajo basket by weaving strips of construction paper. For an African tribal mask we made our own masks using buttons and empty spools.

In the fourth grade, I was sick one Friday and begged my older sister to bring home my art assignment. It was Vincent van Gogh's *Starry Night*. The assignment was to extend the painting to a drawing 8½-by-11 inches. I glued the postcard in the center, and looking at my crayons, sadly decided they could not possibly measure up to the task. I began by

Illustration of a tower by Melissa Newcomb, a seventh-grade student at King Middle School in Portland, Maine.

154

drawing a sketch in pencil and noticed that I would be unable to use my usual pointy stars: van Gogh's stars were lines of concentric circles. By carefully studying van Gogh's painting and creating a convincing expansion of it, I committed it to the ocean bed of my memory.

The first time I visited the Museum of Modern Art in New York City as an adult, I stepped into the room with the original *Starry Night* and its brilliant indigo nearly knocked me over. I recognized this dear old friend I had never met in person. No introduction was necessary.

The world-renowned public preschools in Reggio Emilia, Italy, are noted for their exceptionally close attention to the visual environment. Students' finished work is hung, matted, and displayed as in an art gallery. Student work in progress is also displayed alongside an explanation of the learning process. The natural world is abundantly evident as are reproductions of great works of art. There is nothing in between—no turkey cut-outs, no cereal ads.

As a child I had brief glimpses of what Reggio Emilia's schools offer their students. My teachers did not think me too young to meet Chagall, or too young to cultivate my visual intelligence and imagination.

Often when I visit schools today, I try to imagine myself a student there. If I were sitting at that seat, what would I see all day, every day? Walking down this hallway, what is the visual message I would receive? Whom would my teachers introduce me to via posters, books, and postcards?

Megan Carrie, a seventh-grade student at King Middle School in Portland, Maine, drew this figure as part of an art lesson on texture.

"The whole world is my oyster," the writer Zora Neale Hurston said. We want to give the world to each of our students. Let's be sure we are handing them pearls. ◆

Meg Campbell is the executive director of Expeditionary Learning Outward Bound, and codirector of the Harvard Outward Bound Project at the Harvard Graduate School of Education.